MASTERY

MASTERY

A Mission Plan for Reclaiming a Life
of Purpose, Fitness, and Achievement

Robert Gandt
and
Gary A. Scott

MASTERY: **A Mission Plan for Reclaiming a Life of Purpose, Fitness, and Achievement.**

Dominus Press
Mastery/Robert Gandt and Gary A. Scott 1st ed.

Table of Contents

Part Five: The Anti-Retirement

Part Six: Embracing the New

Part One

The Mastery Manifesto

One can have no smaller or greater
mastery than mastery of oneself.
— LEONARDO DA VINCI

ROBERT GANDT AND GARY A. SCOTT

1

Something is Missing

You know the feeling. It hits you an hour before dawn. You're lying awake in the darkness. A nagging uneasiness has settled on you like a fever. You can't put a name to it or locate the source of the feeling. You only know that something isn't right.

Something is missing.

Life ought to be sweet. You're retired. On permanent vacation. Life is supposed to be carefree. And it is, sort of. You can't help worrying about money. Or, more precisely, running out of moncy. Two recessions, an imploded real estate market, and a capricious stock market have done a number on your net worth. Your income stream has dwindled.

And your health. . . well, it's on a par with your contemporaries. Same elevated blood pressure, cholesterol, joint problems. Standard senior stuff. That's what meds are for, right? It gives you something to talk about at lunch.

You passed on the hardball stuff—running, free weights, singles tennis, high-energy aerobics.   Had to preserve the knees, shoulders, heart. A few rounds of golf and a Sunday walk are enough. Granted, that paunch and jowly jaw weren't in the photo the day you handed in the ID card, peeled your name from the office door, drove out of the parking lot.

You headed into retirement like a stranger into a strange land. The mantra was *stay busy*. Keep yourself occupied. Take the obligatory cruise, visit the relatives, hit the parks, see the shows, spend time with the grandkids. Your days filled with busyness—errands, social events, yard work, games, lunch with friends, fixing things around the house, checking email, forwarding stuff to friends. It was a shared joke: before you retired, how did you ever find time to work?

One day folded into the next, leaving scarcely a trace. Months passed. Years. Time swept around you like the water of a fast-running stream. And sometimes in a reflective moment you wondered:

Where did it go?

What did it mean?

Why do I have this feeling that something is missing?

It's more than a feeling. The uneasiness you sense is real and justified. Something *is* missing. You haven't identified it because it's an intangible, nearly indefinable part of the life that you left behind.

It's called *mission*. Without a mission, your energy, brainpower, and creative spirit are being dispersed like chaff in the wind. You are operating on a level far below your optimum plateau.

To have a mission is to have purpose. Direction. A set of goals. Human beings of every age and disposition—civic volunteers, soldiers, greeters, teachers, astronauts, corporate chiefs, caregivers, truck drivers, writers—function at their highest level when they have a mission.

And so will you. With a mission—and a mission plan—you will attain a new level of performance. You will learn new skills, become physically and mentally stronger, perform at a level higher than you ever believed possible. You will become an advanced human being. You will be on the road to Mastery.

That Old Feeling

The road to Mastery is a long and winding route. The path is lined with waypoints, forks, obstacles. Along the way choices must be made, commitments honored, promises kept. Particularly the promises you make to yourself. As you progress on this journey, you will observe changes in yourself. You may discover that you can do things you thought were out of your reach.

4

MASTERY

These might include:

— recapturing the physical fitness and mental agility you believed were lost forever.

— starting a business that provides a steady income stream and restores your creative spirit.

— becoming fluent in the foreign language you believed only kids could learn.

— recovering muscle mass that you've lost as you've aged, despite what you've been told.

— writing the novel, memoir, or how-to book you've secretly dreamed about—and see it published and sold.

— learning to meditate, recharge, and revitalize your brain and body.

— acquiring new skills: photography, computers, martial arts, oil painting, chess, cooking.

— running, riding road bikes, swimming in the ocean, climbing a mountain.

— learning the piano, guitar, saxophone, or any musical instrument you choose.

— reading 1000+ words a minute and retain what you learn.

— learning to fly, scuba dive, dance, juggle, kick box.

— memorizing entire pages of text, strings of numbers, lists of names.

And at some point in your journey a realization will strike you. That nagging uneasiness that used to settle over you in the pre-dawn darkness? It's gone. It's been replaced by another sensation. One you'd almost forgotten. *That old feeling.* It's the feeling from years ago when the world was fresh and nothing seemed beyond your reach. It's that ready-for-action surge you had when your feet hit the floor in the morning. That kickass feeling when you headed out the door for a five mile run. That heady, take-no-prisoners exultation you sensed when you *knew* you were going to close the deal before you walked into a meeting. The blissful satisfaction that warmed your tired body when you crossed the finish line of the long race.

You remember it. The feeling of empowerment. Independence. Self-determination. Fulfillment. It's still there, and you can get it back.

But you have questions, you say. Let's get them out of the way.

FAQs About Mastery

Q: Learning a language, an instrument, a new skill is *hard*. I'm retired. Why should I spend my energy doing something hard?

A: Because doing that which is hard, whether it's mental or physical, is how you grow. In exercising you gain strength only by stressing your muscles. Likewise, your cognitive powers grow only when they are challenged. Given no challenge, your body and brain atrophy.

Q: Why should I risk heart attack, injury, or joint damage at my age?

A: Life is a risk at any age. You may have an accident. You could crash your bike, break a bone, overstress your body. Certain exertions may not be appropriate for your joints or your back or your heart—*regardless* of your age. You should consider the merits of any undertaking, seek counsel, listen to your physician—and then make your own decision. You—and no one else—have the final say about risk. Once you embrace that precept it becomes an energizing, sometimes scary, liberating life force.

Q: Life is short. At my age, why should I waste my remaining time learning a new—[fill in the blank: *language, musical instrument, sport . . .*]?

A: Because life *is* short. The days will pass at exactly the same rate whether you grow your repertoire of skills or allow your brain and body to remain idle. You can make each day count by striving toward a goal, whether it's becoming stronger, smarter, or just more fulfilled.

Q: My wife, my friends, my kids tell me to "act my age." What is the appropriate response?

A: Smile. You know something they don't know. You *are* acting your age, which, for your purposes, happens to be a state of mind, not a number.

Q: My life is already busy. Where would I find more time for learning a language or training for a sport?

A: You have the same amount of time you've always had: twenty-four hours per day. The way it's spent is your choice. The first step toward Mastery is identifying your mission. The next step is committing to that mission. Eliminate what's not important and reallocate. More about that later.

Q: How will I know when it's time to quit— [fill in the blank: *running, traveling, flying . . .]?*

A: "Quit" is an absolute, implying a fixed demarcation between doing something and not doing it. The bias of Mastery is toward *doing*. With all passions and pursuits, you will tailor what you do to match your evolving reality. Quit flying? Not so fast. The time will come when you step down from the cockpit of a high performance aircraft—but you can still go flying in a light sport airplane. An Ironman competition? Maybe not realistic for your age and condition—but perhaps you can train for a sprint triathlon. Or a 10K run. Or a cross-state bike ride. Climb to the summit of Kilimanjaro? Perhaps not, but you could make the trek to Machu Picchu. Or hike the Appalachian Trail. Take our word for it, the view is just as spectacular.

2

What is Mastery?

In its simplest definition, Mastery is the process of becoming an advanced human being. Though Mastery is an ageless concept, it has special implications for the vast segment of our population we call "seniors." That broad category includes the eighty-five million Boomers—the post-World War II generation now entering elderhood—as well as their predecessors from the 1920s, 1930s, and early 1940s. The principles of Mastery also have meaning for the Gen-Xers—post-Boomers embarked on their second half-century.

Mastery is about making the rest of your life meaningful. It is a state of being, not a curriculum. The pursuit of Mastery means growing, exploring, advancing. It can also mean leaving an old life behind.

And this, we fully understand, is not for everyone. A sizeable number of seniors will declare in a loud voice that their current life suits them just fine, thank you. No change requested or required. They happen to be living precisely the life style they always anticipated for their golden years, coasting out in sublime, stress-free bliss. Never mind challenges, explorations, advancements. Life is sweet and ought not to be changed.

To them we say, God bless. We salute you and suggest that you gently close this book and resume living a joyful existence. What follows is for the rest of you—a minority who sense that life may be slipping past you. That something truly *is* missing.

In the chapters to come you will find a compendium of methods and suggestions to insert purpose into your daily life. Not all will be suitable for you. Some you will find unacceptably difficult or beyond your comfort level or simply not to your taste. The eighty-year-old athlete may not choose the same fitness regimen as her fifty-year-old running mates. The financially secure retiree may not be interested in founding a new micro-business. The physically handicapped senior may quite understandably opt out of high-intensity weight training.

Their reasoning is correct. The purpose of Mastery is *not* to compromise your health, place you in danger, or sacrifice your quality of life. Precisely the opposite. The core principle of Mastery is to expand your personal envelope in the pursuit of sensible, executable missions. As you achieve your objectives you will be rewarded with the knowledge that you and you alone are the master of your fate.

The Mission

mission: (noun) 1. an important goal or purpose that is accompanied by strong conviction.
—Oxford Dictionary

The journey to Mastery begins with a mission. Defining your mission is the first step in declaring your independence. It is the concept of mission that puts purpose and structure back into your daily existence. When life's inevitable storms throw you off course, your commitment to your mission will steer you back to your true direction.

But what, precisely, is a mission?

In recent times the classic word "mission" has received fuzzy new meanings. When applied to a corporation or agency, it usually implies some long term result or condition. In consultant-speak a mission plan is a statement of direction and values. A mission plan can serve as an institutional compass.

For you, a traveler on the road to Mastery, mission means something else. It is a process of achievement. The operative word here is *process*. Your focus is on *doing* rather than *being*.

MASTERY

A mission has a beginning and an end. It has a strategy, measurable stages of accomplishment, and a time frame. A mission requires a commitment you make to yourself.

A mission isn't a vague, mystical path to some higher plateau. It's not answering a call to serve God or save the planet or seek higher meaning, though those can be aspects of any mission. A mission *can* be grand in scale—to become President, found a new industry, find a cure for cancer—but the missions we describe in *Mastery* are more finite and available to everyone: learning a language; achieving an athletic benchmark; writing a book; learning a new culture through travel; starting a micro-business.

Though your mission will have a defined objective, your primary focus of attention will be on the *journey* to that objective, not on the ultimate condition. Mastery may be considered the sum total of *all* your missions.

For example, assume you have assigned yourself the mission of learning Spanish. Fulfilling the mission—in this case attaining fluency in Español—is not an end in itself. It's not a checked-off credential like a school diploma that you hang on your wall to impress visitors. For you this completed mission is an entry point for a new mission. With your freshly acquired skill you are prepared to explore new countries, understand foreign cultures, learn *another* language, acquire knowledge in a way that was not possible before. Your mission is a waypoint on your journey to becoming an advanced human being.

ROBERT GANDT AND GARY A. SCOTT

Defining the Mission

The object of your mission is to explore the Missouri River & such principal stream of it, as, by its course and communication with the waters of the Pacific Ocean may offer the most direct & practicable water communication across this continent for the purpose of commerce.
 — PRESIDENT THOMAS JEFFERSON, June, 1803, defining the mission of Lewis and Clark

Your mission, should you choose to accept it. . .
—from the 1960's television series "Mission Impossible."

As a kid you had dreams. Big dreams. You indulged in fantasies. Some were so over the top you kept them to yourself like a secret treasure. Nothing was beyond the limit of your imagination. If you were a boy you flew spaceships, fought crime, punched out thugs, won the heart of the pig-tailed girl in the row ahead of you in the fifth grade, saved the world from aliens, pitched a no-hitter in the World Series. If you were a girl you trounced your classmates (boys and girls) in sports as well as academics, appeared in heart-wrenching cinema epics, ran a mega-business from your glamorous penthouse, took dawn rides on your prize stallion along a Mediterranean beach, wrote a best-selling novel about love in the apocalypse, played the violin to a spellbound audience at Carnegie Hall.

Dreaming was fun and harmless. No stigma attached. You could insert yourself into any role and *see* yourself being a winner. A superstar. You were your own hero.

And then something happened. Years passed. The dreams faded. You grew up. Your grand imaginings were shunted into a dark closet of your mind like a stack of forbidden comics. Too far-fetched, too embarrassing, too phantasmagorical for the adult world.

It's time to revisit those dreams. Let's dig through your closet of nearly-forgotten fantasies. What was that feat you imagined accomplishing before the image faded away like an illusion? What was that fondest daydream, the one that kept inserting itself into your idle thoughts? Keep digging. You may be surprised to discover that some of those childhood yearnings are still alive.

In them lie the foundation for your mission.

Begin the search for your mission by tapping your inner core. Enter a relaxed, meditative state (more about his technique later). Be a child again. Dust off your long-suppressed dreams, identify your oldest, most urgent yearnings, give them a fresh viewing. You may find that at least one of those old fantasies still smolders inside you, beckoning like an ancient spirit.

That childhood dream you had about writing the great American novel? Is the dream still there? In real life you didn't write the novel, or anything else. Time and self-doubt and the demands of making a living got in the way. But there it is, still residing in your core like a hidden yearning.

Is this a valid mission?

Consider your other old fantasies. Perhaps you imagined sprinting across the finish line at the Olympics, winning a gold medal. It was pure silliness, of course, because you never competed in a race, Olympic or otherwise. You had neither the body type or the inclination for such activity. But there it is anyway, that old kernel of a dream, nestled in your memory. How does it make you feel? Does getting into shape, hitting the road, setting yourself the goal of competing in a future event appeal to you?

Are you sensing a mission?

Or that violin performance at Carnegie Hall. As it turned out you never actually picked up a violin, or any other instrument. Someone—a parent, teacher, friend—told you that you had no gift for music. You believed them. The fantasy joined your other forgotten fantasies in the darkened closet. Life marched on. But here you are several decades later, digging through the bin of discarded dreams, and you discover—*voila!* — that secret fantasy. There it lies, like a forgotten photograph. And something about it stirs that old yearning inside you.

Could this be a mission?

Your mission can be a grandly ambitious, long-haul project, such as founding a business enterprise that will continue to grow after you're gone. Or it can be a short-range, attainable objective like training for and completing a 10-K race. Or learning a new skill such as juggling or woodworking. What's critical is that you define the mission. Do the homework. Determine the steps required, the waypoints you intend to pass. Ask questions, consult experts, gather the information you need before you begin.

Let's say your mission is to learn a language. First set the bar. Establish what level of competency you seek. Do you want to communicate on a conversational level with native speakers? To read and write the language? To learn enough to travel within a foreign country without speaking English? To pass a competency test for academic credit? To qualify for an overseas-based job?

Okay, you've chosen your target level. Now check out the available ways to learn the language. You could sign up for formal classes. You could hire a private tutor. You could choose one of the many interactive computer or software courses. You could immerse totally by living in a country while taking language instruction. Or you could put together a package of several of these options. Pick your method, and you'll have accomplished the first step of your mission.

And now the second step.

Put it in Writing

I am indebted to my notebook for the happiness of my whole life.
—BENJAMIN FRANKLIN at age 79

Writing is thinking. This is another of the core tenets of Mastery. The process of writing about your mission compels you to reflect on what you're doing and why you're doing it. Writing about progress toward a goal provides clarity and understanding. For this reason we urge you to keep a notebook. Or, even better, multiple notebooks. In them you'll store those parcels of knowledge you obtain from your research. You'll record progress—

in the way a captain keeps a ship's log—of your mission. And this is where you'll stash your mission plan.

What's that? You don't have a mission plan? We'll come back to that, but for now just know that *every* mission, like every journey, is best fulfilled by following a plan, including our hypothetical mission to learn a new language.

Your notebook can be in any form. For the tech-oriented there is the digital option, using any of several note-keeping computer programs. The best are those that can be synched across platforms so that your notes are up to date whichever machine you're on. Most have password protection so that none of your data is compromised.

For Windows users there are numerous excellent apps, including Microsoft OneNote, a killer note-taking program that integrates with every corner of the PC. Evernote is a free, cross-platform universal capture application, also available on Mac. Others are Omnifocus, Trello, ActionMethod, or Basecamp.

Mac types are well served by Circus Ponies NoteBook, a powerful app that manages notes as well as organizes projects and collects multi-media files. MacJournal is what it implies—a slick journaling program that organizes your entries and displays them logically. For both Mac and Windows is Scrivener, a powerful content-generation tool particularly suited for writers and researchers. Also for Mac is a robust app called WriteRoom, that presents a minimalist interface that eliminates screen distractions.

But there's another option. In the tradition of Leonardo da Vinci and Benjamin Franklin, you can do your note-keeping the old-fashioned way with a pen and notebook. Da Vinci kept voluminous notebooks in which he recorded not only the ideas that streaked like meteorites through his mind, he inserted masterful sketches of inventions, art conceptions, and detailed etchings of the human anatomy.

So did Benjamin Franklin, a prototypical student of Mastery. Franklin's notebook went with him everywhere, and in it he recorded his progress toward his ultimate goal of attaining thirteen specific virtues. Another famous note taker was Thomas Jefferson, who rose early each morning wherever he was in the world to record his observations of weather, bird migrations, and musings about geography and politics. Ernest Hemingway always carried a notebook in which he wrote impressions of people, battles, sights and smells, the chaos and richness of life that became the substance of his novels. Ludwig von Beethoven used his notebooks as musical sketchbooks for capturing inspirations about literature and music. So did Charles Darwin, filling his notebooks with jottings about everything from zoology, archeology, shopping lists, and family matters.[1]

Your notebook can be as fancy or utilitarian as you wish. You can go for one of the classic notebooks from Moleskine, whose journals, they claim, were used by Hemingway. For carrying around, there's nothing better than the pocket-sized Moleskine Cahier notebooks, which have stiff cardboard covers and sell in packs of three. For a larger format suitable for your desk or backpack, try one of the 9 ¾X7 ½ student's ruled composition notebook from any office supply store. The composition books from Staples come in packs of two. They're stiff-backed, transportable, and imminently suitable for journaling and storing your voluminous mission notes.

Why take notes at all? Because with most missions, note-taking will be an inherent part of the process. Over the years multiple studies have proven the connection between note-taking and learning. More recent research has focused on whether hand-writing engages a different part of the brain than when using a keyboard.

Remember those voluminous notes you took during college lectures? The truth was, the taking of notes had less to do with recording highlights of the lecture than it did with the engagement of your brain. The act of writing in your notebook formed the neural connection that helped you recall the information for the coming exam.

Writing by Hand

In this digital age, writing by hand may seem like a stone age skill you no longer require. In fact cursive—basic handwriting—is no longer taught in many elementary classrooms in the U. S. The current thinking seems to be that beyond signing their name and printing block letters when necessary, future adults will convert thoughts to symbols exclusively with a keyboard.

Perhaps. But in the process they will be losing something important. Research supports the theory that writing by hand engages the brain in a different way than by using a keyboard. Virginia Berninger,[2] a professor of educational psychology at the University of Washington, says handwriting differs from typing because it requires executing sequential strokes to form a letter, whereas keyboarding involves selecting a whole letter by touching a key. The act of writing by hand on a conventional paper pad has the effect of loosening the flow of thoughts, permitting a freer association of ideas. Handwriting seems to invoke a more direct association with the creative regions of our brains.[3] Berninger's studies also showed that children who wrote by hand versus a keyboard wrote more words, faster, and expressed more ideas.

It's not a new idea. The philosopher Martin Heidegger abhorred the impersonalized typewriter keyboard: "Mechanized writing deprives the hand of dignity in the realm of the written word and degrades the word into a mere means for the traffic of communication. Besides, mechanized writing offers the advantage of covering up one's handwriting and therewith one's character."[4]

Technology may be rendering handwriting obsolete, but it also offers new twists on an ancient skill. Several apps are available to enable handwriting on mobile devices like the iPad and iPhone, including WritePad, which has built-in handwriting recognition software, and straight handwriting apps like Notability, Penultimate, and Noteshelf.

Is it too late to resume handwriting? Like all unused skills, your handwriting may have deteriorated to an illegible scrawl over the decades. There are programs to recover and improve this basic skill. Nan Barchowsky, for one, sells an excellent program (paper, of course) called FIX IT...WRITE, which includes sections for both print script and cursive handwriting.

Make technology your friend, but at the same time maintain the vital connection between your brain and your hands. Writing in your notebook—paper or digital—is an exercise in reflection and meditation. Your fingers become an extension of your mind. Let them trace the route to your destination—Mastery.

---

[1] The Art of Manliness is a lively blog with musings not only about the use of the pocket notebook but thoughts about fitness, survival, and grooming. Despite the name, it's not just for men.

[2] Professor Berninger says pictures of the brain have illustrated that sequential finger movements activated massive regions involved in thinking, language and working memory—the system for temporarily storing and managing information. *Wall Street Journal Oct. 5 2010*.

[3] In one study, fMRI (functional Magnetic Resonance Imaging) data showed that processing the orientation of handwritten and typed characters did not rely on the same brain areas. Greater activity related to handwriting learning was observed in several brain regions known to be involved in the execution, imagery, and observation of actions. *Advances in Haptics*. http://www.intechopen.com/articles/show/title/digitizing -literacy-reflections-on-the-haptics-of-writing.

4 Philosopher Martin Heidegger (1889-1976) was a controversial figure mainly for his affiliation with Nazism, for which he never expressed regret.

3

The Mission Plan

You've chosen your mission. The next step is to define the mission in terms of *what* you plan to achieve. This is where your intentions transform from a fuzzy whim to a clearly envisioned objective. Whether you write in a notebook or a digital format, use this phase to reflect on the nature of your upcoming mission. Fix in your mind the destination at the end of your journey. Be specific, and be realistic. Your objective must be measurable.

If, for example, your goal is to learn a foreign language, determine *what* level of proficiency you expect to attain. Fluency for a non-native speaker ranges from novice level to intermediate to advanced (these classifications are arbitrary; schools and agencies apply different parameters to language fluency). If your mission is to reach the intermediate level, then your definition might specify a basic vocabulary of at least 2,000 words, the ability to understand and express yourself in present, past, and future tenses, the competence to travel unassisted in a native-language environment.

With the objective clearly defined, determine what steps must be taken to get there. Do your homework. Should you take a course? Acquire a tutor? Immerse yourself in a native-language environment? Or, given a background in learning languages, can you go it alone by deconstructing the language to its essential elements and building your own foundation ("meta-learning" as Tim Ferriss, serial language learner, suggests in *The Four-Hour Chef*)?

Choose your route and lay it out in your mission plan, step by step, like a sequential map to your destination. Identify the critical waypoints. These waypoints not only mark your progress, they provide the gratification of intermediate goals attained. The passage of each waypoint is an opportunity to reward yourself, accept congratulations, then push on.

A mission plan to learn a language might include these en route waypoints:

— Elementary vocabulary; ability to construct spontaneous simple sentences.

— Express and understand spoken and written compound sentences.

— Competence with grammar—past, future, and imperfect tenses.

— Ability to sustain everyday dialogue with native speakers

Keep in mind that the route to your destination, like all routes, is subject to detour. You may encounter roadblocks, storms, unfriendly terrain. You may discover a more direct path. Not to worry. You can navigate past all such contingencies because you'll have in your hand the essential guidebook—your mission plan.

The Timeline

It is not that we have a short space of time, but that we waste much of it. Life is long enough, and it has been given in sufficiently generous measure to allow the accomplishment of the very greatest things if the whole of it is well invested.
—SENECA, *On the Shortness of Life*

The mission plan is not complete until you apply a timeline. This is the crucial difference between pursuing a mission and simply engaging in an activity with an open-ended window of accomplishment. Applying a timeline inserts accountability. Are you on track? Ahead of schedule? Falling behind? Aviators call this a "Howgozit"—a visual measuring stick of their progress over the earth. We call it a mission plan.

As in an aviator's flight plan you determine an ETA—estimated time of arrival—for each waypoint as well as the destination. Again, be realistic. What is your expected rate of progress? If you've learned a language previously, or trained for an event like a triathlon or a mountain climb, you know how long the process ought to take. Make the schedule reasonable—and doable.

Without the accountability of a time-oriented mission plan, you drift in a sea of good intentions. Those grand aspirations to learn a language, achieve a level of fitness, acquire a new skill somehow go unfulfilled. They get lost in a messy basket of activities that have no defined outcome. Months and then years slip past. Those dreamed-of goals never become reality. This describes the condition of the vast majority of boomers, retirees, and senior adults who fill their lives with busyness—chores, games, meetings, television, and perhaps even the pursuit of a new skill. For them time is a reservoir from which they can draw endlessly. Someday they'll get around to *really* learning that language. Someday they'll be *really* fit. Someday they'll *really* learn to play that instrument.

Except for the small fragment of our population who are self-directed and highly disciplined achievers, "someday" is a bogus promise.

The seeker of Mastery knows better. He understands that time is a precious and finite asset.

4

Resistance

We have met the enemy and he is us.
—POGO (cartoon character created by Walt Kelly)

Here's a reality: the path to Mastery is not a smooth route. You'll have to come to terms with that reality soon after you've made the commitment to your mission. Understand that you *will* encounter resistance, and it will take many forms. Your body will balk, and so will your brain. You will feel alone, cut off from the world you formerly inhabited. You will have to become your own head coach. Your own cheering section. Your own hero.

There is no end to the forms resistance can take. You'll be besieged by distractions, all competing for the vital energy and time you must devote to your mission. Television, social engagements, email, the internet, magazines—a plethora of time-wasters. The pursuit of Mastery means becoming a master of your own life and time. *You*—not the magazine editors, television producers, junk-mailers, email-forwarders, idle telephoners and texters—must choose what commands your attention. Remember the mantra: *Life is short.*

Resistance will come from unexpected places. People who claim to have your best interests at heart—your spouse, your best friend, your contemporaries—will issue warnings, ridicule, even outright hostility.

Why is this?

Because a subtle human social trait reveals itself. Though your well-intentioned family and friends *do* wish you well, they don't want you to change, at least in a way that defies their own beliefs. Your contemporaries may feel threatened seeing that you're spending your account—the finite substance called time—differently than they are. Call it the crab-in-the-bucket syndrome, where the crabs collectively keep any single crab from escaping. Or call it consensus thinking, all of them deciding they know better than you what's good for you.

They don't.

But your severest opposition will come from an invisible—and familiar—adversary. He is vicious and tenacious. Over and over his voice repeats itself like a drumbeat: *You're too old. . . You can't do that. . . You shouldn't even think like that. . . You're not ready for this stuff. . . It's too late for you. . . You'll be a laughing stock. . . You'll make an ass of yourself. . . Your friends will think you've gone off the rails. . . You'll get hurt. . . You'll be sorry you tried that.*

And, worst of all . . . *You'll fail.*

Shut out the noise. What you're hearing is the voice of the enemy. Slam the door on him. He's a liar and a fraud. He wants nothing more than to keep you locked up in the prison of your self-imposed limitations. He wants you to keep believing the lies.

Bright Shining Lies

You know them. You've been hearing them since you entered adulthood. Over the years, as you passed from one life stage to the next, these bright shining lies have taken on the obdurate quality of truth.

Let's treat them for what they are: lies. They are the language of the enemy. Let's dispel some of them.

> *Lie #1: Only kids can . . .* [fill in the blank: *learn a language, musical instrument, martial arts*]. It's true that children's brains are different. In certain ways they absorb information more adeptly. In some circumstances their cognitive functions are quicker. In other ways, *you* possess

the advantage. You have better discipline. You can perceive patterns based on the knowledge you've acquired about what works and what doesn't. You have organizational skills that allow you to prioritize the processes of learning. The challenge is in freeing your brain from its myth-based beliefs. Open up, let it flow, have fun. With the correct mindset, you can learn at a greater rate than ever before in your life.

Lie #2: *You can't build muscle mass after the age of* . . . [fill in the blank: *forty, fifty, sixty, beyond*]. This is one of the more destructive myths. While it's true that at about age 30 you begin to lose muscle mass, here's the pertinent fact: *muscle mass is restorable.* In fact, as you enter your senior years it becomes more critical than ever to *build* muscle. Your muscle mass is vital in preserving strength, vitality, and resistance to infirmity. And you can build muscle *at any age.* More about this in *Part Two: Getting Physical.*

Lie #3: *Sex is over at the age of* . . . [fill in the blank: *sixty, seventy, eighty* . . .] As with every other mental and physical activity, a healthy sex life depends on overall mind-body fitness. According to Sue Goldstein, sexuality educator and program coordinator for San Diego Sexual Medicine, sexual interest and activity is not age-based. "We have patients as young as 18 and as old as 90 coming to be treated so they can once again enjoy a satisfying sexual life."[1] The truth? Sex can be even *more* exciting and satisfying with age. Libido for both men and women is a function more of health and desire than of age. It's not over until it's over.

Lie #4: *Technology has passed me by. It's too late for me to learn* ... [fill in the blank: *computers, e-books, online marketing, robotics*]. Most professional skills of the future—yes, *your* future—will have some connection to computer science. And you already possess the aptitude to learn these skills, even if you don't yet believe it. Evidence suggests that learning computer skills is akin to learning a foreign language. Says Michael Ullman, director of the Brain and Language Lab at Georgetown University Medical Center, "I ²would speculate that the same general-purpose memory systems that underlie language learning in children and adults likely underlie the learning of computer languages." As in Myth #1, the challenge is not *whether* you can learn new technology, but how you go about it. Open yourself to fresh concepts, new terminology, unfamiliar devices. Let your mind be a sponge. Become childlike. Play, roll with it, experiment. And—this is a promise—you *will* learn.

Lie #5: *I'm too old to* ... [fill in the blank: *learn to fly, write a book, climb mountains, learn computers* . .]. This is an offshoot of Myth #1 wherein you accept that any skills not acquired when you were young are forever denied to you. To believe this myth, you must also accept that you have reached a stasis in life, no longer capable of growth or change. Nothing could be further from the truth. You are an evolving specimen, a work in progress. The only stasis is in your willingness to grow. The acquisition of new skills in your senior years is not only possible, it is essential in your progress toward Mastery.

The Someday Syndrome

You've heard the statement a thousand times. Almost daily you hear it repeated by someone you know. Most of all, you hear it from yourself. The statement begins with *Someday* — and it has an infinite number of endings. You know them all by heart. *Someday I'll . . .*

> *. . . learn French.*
> *. . . start a foundation to combat homelessness.*
> *. . . hike the Appalachian Trail.*
> *. . . play the saxophone.*
> *. . . join an archeological expedition in Jordan.*
> *. . . finish the memoir I promised myself I'd write.*
> *. . . found a thriving e-business.*

Someday. It's the great sinkhole that consumes your grandest aspirations. The Someday Syndrome has the power of an addictive drug, allowing you to *imagine* achieving your goal without actually having to do it. It tempts you with perfectly plausible excuses *not* to begin your mission.

You know the excuses. They usually begin with *I'll get around to it . . .*

> *. . . when I have more time.*
> *. . . when I have more money.*
> *. . . when I feel more motivated.*
> *. . . when I've —[fill in the blank: remodeled the kitchen, visited the kids, finished the golf season, lost twenty pounds . . .]*

Of all the enemies you will confront on the road to Mastery, the Someday Syndrome is the most insidious. It offers comfort in the form of syrupy affirmations. Yes, it assures you, you *could* attain your goal—anytime you choose. Yes, of course, you're going to get around to it—later. And certainly, the mission is worth doing—but not just yet. *Someday.*

The seeker of Mastery knows better. "Someday" is a blurry abstraction that has no applicability in the pursuit of Mastery. It can mean next week, next year, or never. To the aspiring Master, the dimension of time is a measurable and finite asset. Life *is* short. Forget Someday.

Easily said, but the syndrome is nonetheless real and deadly. So why *do* human beings procrastinate? Why *do* we dodge and weave and sidestep the commitment to our mission?

The primary reason is fear. Fear of making a choice. Fear of change. Fear of failing. The list of fears is endless. As a seeker of Mastery you must understand that you can only advance toward the next plateau by confronting these fears.

You confront them by asking questions. By keeping yourself honest. Write the questions down. Then answer them, one at a time.

— *What am I risking?*

Give it serious consideration and weigh the risk versus the reward. Will this endanger your life? Could it cause a change in your marriage, relationship, social status? Can you live with any of these alterations? Could you repair the damage? Would you?

— *What is the worst thing that could happen?*

Visualize one possible calamitous consequence. Then another. Think of as many as you can. Give yourself a wide-eyed view of all the grim scenarios. Imagine each one happening. Often, what you fear the most is that which you don't know. Most, you will probably discover, are boogeymen. You can tell yourself, okay, I know these boogeymen for what they are. They can't surprise me.

— *What is the best thing that could happen?*

Envision the brightest, happiest outcome to your mission. Imagine the sweet taste of success as you reach your goal. Let this be your motivational image. Let the image power you past your fear.

— *Why am I not taking action?*

Which particular fear is blocking your way? Identify it. Is it a physical danger? Is it the possible loss of money, assets, time? Is it fear of failure? Fear of embarrassment? Fear of being in over your head? Reflect on previous confrontations with your fears. Remember those occasions when you made the tough calls, quit the bad habits, took preemptive action against a looming threat. Remember the feeling of having done something that you feared. Remember that feeling of empowerment. It's still there, waiting for you to claim it.

According to an old adage, that which we fear the most is often that which we ought to be doing. Advancing to a new and better life means confronting that fear. It means making a tough decision. It could mean leaving an old life behind. It means commitment.

The Big C

The moment one definitely commits oneself, then providence moves too. A whole stream of events issues from the decision, raising in one's favor all manner of unforeseen incidents, meetings and material assistance, which no man could have dreamt would have come his way.
—W. H. MURRAY, leader of the Scottish Himalayan Mountain Expedition

You have a mission plan. You've identified the intermediate waypoints, and you've applied a timeline. Now pause to reflect. Will the accomplishment be worthy of your most focused energy? Does it conform to your own inner core values? Is this mission compatible with your existing commitments?

This is the time to exercise discretion. In their zeal to reach a higher plateau, seekers of Mastery may be tempted to take on multiple simultaneous missions. The result is that they fragment their precious time and concentration. They scatter their energy like a shower of sparks across the spectrum, and in the process they become dilettantes—dabblers at an agenda of pursuits instead of focusing their vital attention on the most important mission.

In this age of multitasking and hyper-frenetic appointment-making, less is often more. One of the essential elements of Mastery is focus. Staying on point, resisting distractions, eliminating the unessential. If in the heady stage of mission-building you took on the simultaneous tasks of learning Chinese, training for a triathlon, writing a memoir, trekking across Mongolia, taking up the zither, piano, and saxophone, reading the entire works of Shakespeare, earning a black belt in karate, launching an e-business, you would either be inordinately ambitious or delusional. In either case the route to Mastery would be an impossible maze. You would be a hopeless dilettante.

Take the time to give the proposed mission your closest scrutiny. Enter a relaxed, meditative state and visualize what will be required. Be painfully honest. Can you maintain your focus and exuberance on this task? Does it feel right for you? Will the outcome be worth the expense of time and energy? If the answer is yes, then you're ready for the launch pad. The Big Commit.

Commitment is the dam buster. It gives definition to an undefined mission, clarity to the cloudy picture. Commitment provides direction. With commitment, you *know* at any time where you're supposed to be and where you're going.

Something potent happens when you make the Big Commit. You are imbued with a new energy. A sense of empowerment. You can feel it coursing through your veins like an elixir.

Savor this feeling. Store it in a place where you can summon it back. You'll need it when the road ahead steepens and headwinds resist your progress. Recall that surge of enthusiasm when you made the Big C. It will be your reserve strength when the time comes that you need it.

And that time *will* come.

Staying Committed

There is no chance, no destiny, no fate, that can circumvent or hinder or control the firm resolve of a determined soul.
—ELLA WHEELER WILCOX

Inevitably the sweet glow of mission launch wears off. You don't feel like sustaining the same day-after-day level of intensity. Fatigue, self-doubt, and yes, boredom from the repetitive activity sets in. Your progress in learning Russian hits a limit that feels like a dead end. Your goal to compete in that century bike race seems more and more a fool's errand. Playing "Moonlight Sonata" in a public recital has become a fanciful delusion.

A chorus of negative comments swells up around you. *Are you crazy? Why are you wasting time/money/energy on that? You could be playing golf.* And, of course, the oldest line in the litany: *Act your age.*

But the most stinging rebuke comes from a familiar source. You hear from the old enemy that Pogo identified as *Us. What was I thinking? Why did I commit to this? What made me think I would stick with something this hard?*

Part of making the Big C—and *staying* committed—is knowing that this will happen. You expect it, then continue on course, putting one foot ahead of the other. You close your ears to the chorus of negativity. Is it easy? Of course not.

Staying committed to the mission requires that you revisit the reasons that compelled you to seek Mastery in the first place. Remember that old feeling you used to have: *Something is missing.* Make yourself recall that solid satisfaction that comes when your life has purpose, direction, structure.

Take a moment to kick back. Meditate, take a long solo walk, or simply relax and close your eyes. Visualize the outcome you desire from your mission. See yourself *being* what you want to be. See yourself *doing* the very thing that you intend to do. Do this often. Make it a part of your daily routine. It will have the effect of refocusing your energy on your objective.

And then write it down.

Remember the Mastery tenet: *Writing is thinking.* The act of recording the progress of your mission has the power to keep you focused. Whether you keep a separate journal or use the same notebook in which you outlined your mission plan, the value of keeping a written accounting of your mission cannot be overemphasized.

The explorers Lewis and Clark chronicled their mission to explore the American West in eighteen handwritten journals. In their journals the explorers recorded observations of weather, geography, native tribes, and entered freehand sketches of animals, plants, canoes, costumes. Clark drew a number of surprisingly accurate maps.

But the explorers' journals did more than document an epic event. The meticulous daily entries were Lewis and Clark's window into their own souls. In their journals they could vent their frustrations, analyze mistakes, make observations about the natives they encountered.

"These are the vilest miscreants of the savage race," Meriwether Lewis wrote about the Teton Sioux, "and must ever remain the pirates of the Missouri until such measures are pursued by our government as will make them feel a dependence on it."[3]

William Clark, though less schooled than Lewis in grammar, was more expressive. After nearly a year and a half of westward journeying, he exclaimed in his journal, "Great joy in camp. We are in View of the Ocian [sic], this great Pacific Ocean which we been So long anxious to See."

Staying committed to a mission, as Lewis and Clark were, is even more difficult when you alone are responsible for the outcome. It means ignoring the tugging and pushing of well-intentioned family members, friends, associates who make claims on your time and energy. It means taking control of your time, eliminating the distractions that you and others have given yourself—the time killers and attention consumers and productivity thieves that sabotage your mission.

Old habits die hard. New ones must be cultivated like seedlings. The same old sirens beckon—the inbox filled with the forwarded emails from your network of friends; the universe of Googled answers to every question; social breakfasts and lunches and cocktail parties filled with empty chatter. And the ultimate of all time sinks, television.

Freeing yourself from the sirens takes a commitment no less specific than that of learning a language or a musical instrument or achieving physical fitness. It means adopting habits of discipline, order, and a work ethic. And it means rejection of the disorderly, distracted, unproductive life style.

Commitment requires that you confront your enemy. You have to go *mano a mano* against the same old adversary time and time again. It's not an easy path. The path of least resistance will not take you where you want to go. Remind yourself that conflict is not only inevitable, it makes you stronger.

---

[1] When twenty-year-old singer Miley Cyrus declared on the *Today* show that people "stop having sex after forty," the statement was greeted with jeers by, among others, author Joan Price, seventy-years old "and not slowing down a heck of a lot." Price is the author of *Naked at Our age: Talking Out Loud about Senior Sex.* http://www.today.com/health/miley-cyrus-says-sex-ends-40-not-true-say-experts-8C11352134

[2] *Wired* magazine, October, 2012, p. 32.

[3] Quoted in Bernard De Voto, *The Course of Empire* (Houghton Mifflin, 1998), 458.

5

Life is Finite (and Short)

Time is the coin of your life. It is the only coin you have, and only you can determine how it will be spent. Be careful lest you let other people spend it for you.
—CARL SANDBURG

For most of your life you've been bombarded with aphorisms: *Time is money. Life is short. Time is the stuff life is made of.* And so on. Along with most such aphorisms, they were filed in your mental trash folder. They seemed irrelevant.

That was then. This is now, and the aphorisms are no longer irrelevant. Life *is* short, and it becomes shorter, day by day.

You have an account, and it's comprised of that essential life substance—time. The balance of the account—the time remaining in your life—is drawn down daily. Each of us—rich, poor, industrial magnate, homeless derelict, super achiever, perennial ne'er do well—draws the same twenty-four hours from his account each day. No more, no less. No trust funds replenishing anyone's squandered account. It's the great equalizer in the otherwise unequal distribution of assets across the human race.

If there is anything good about life in the senior lane, it is this knowledge: *Your account is finite.* It may not be close to zero, but close enough that you can see the bottom line. Remember the blurry years of your youth when you delayed pursuing your grandest dreams? The halcyon days when you could put off anything because there was always more time? Time was an abstract, limitless substance. An infinite number of tomorrows.

No more. Now you know. Time is *not* infinite. Time is precious. Time, unlike money, is irreplaceable. Time spent in front of a television, skimming magazines, surfing the net, reading junk mail, answering marketing calls, doing piddling errands is time lost. Time spent in the company of tiresome and spirit-draining people is time wasted.

Time that slips through your fingers for no desired purpose has vanished forever, leaving scarcely a trace. No matter *how* your time is spent, it is spent. Deducted from your balance. The zeroes on the bottom line are becoming easier to read.

You probably keep careful records of your money flow. You reconcile bank accounts, track investments, monitor expenditures. But rarely do you track the expenditure of your most precious commodity—time—with anywhere the same diligence. When you abruptly realize the lateness of the day, or of the season, or of your life, you ask the inevitable question: *Where did the time go?*

You don't know. It just went. It receded into the distance like the view from a fast-moving train. You had no plan for how to spend it, nor do you have a record of where it went. You are left staring at your depleted balance sheet with only an indistinct memory of what happened.

Or didn't happen.

The first step in taking back control of your life is to account for your time. Let this be the opening shot in your coming war of independence. Begin each day with a WIWTH (What I Want to Happen) list. The WIWTH list is best written the night before. With your most important tasks already identified, you have a jumpstart on the new day.

There is immense power in the WIWTH concept. The knowledge that *you* have taken control of your affairs places you on the leading edge of the day's activities. You become proactive, initiating the events that *you* want to happen instead of reacting to each fresh wave and tremor the world sends your way. It's a win-win for everyone. The benefits of your proactivity extend to everyone who works for you, employs you, depends on you. You will be more productive, make better decisions, keep your actions consistent with your values.

The WIWTH list is not be confused with a traditional To Do or time management list. Your WIWTH list puts the emphasis on the first three letters—*What I want*—which differentiates it from *What The World Wants*—the chores and obligations expected of you by employer and family and society. Your WIWTH list itemizes those outcomes most important to *you*—the urgent desires *you* want fulfilled by the time the day has been deducted from your account.

There are dozens of day planners and time management systems available, paper and digital. A few are good, many are not, but most have one thing in common: they are designed to align *your* schedule with the demands of the world. They accommodate the hour-to-hour needs of harried businessmen and frenetic appointment keepers. And yes, using a time management system—almost any system—is preferable to no management at all of your daily schedule.

But your WIWTH list is not an appointment planner, though you can include such items. The value of the WIWTH list is that it compels you to actually *think* about your most desired outcomes in the coming day. View it as a route map with the important waypoints highlighted. Like any good route map, it provides a look-back as well as a look-forward in your progress to Mastery.

When you fully embrace this new way of viewing your day, you'll hear a satisfying sound: another round fired in your war for personal freedom. The WIWTH list can be a separate record or, even better, it can be part of your journal.

What's that? You don't keep a journal? Then it's time to discuss another subject: the fine art of journal-keeping.

The Examined Life: Journal Keeping and Feedback Loops

There is no such thing in anyone's life as an unimportant day.
—ALEXANDER WOOLLCOTT

On your path to Mastery, you will monitor your time account as faithfully as you do your financial accounts. You will *know* how your time is spent and invested.

How you monitor the account—with your WIWTH list or in a diary-style journal—doesn't matter. The objective remains the same: to provide a look-forward-look-back view of how your time is spent. The process of recording daily data requires you to *think* about how you withdraw time from your account.

And why is this important?

Because life is messy. Seldom do the events of your day sort themselves into neat or logical patterns. The days and years whir past, leaving you with a jumble of impressions that soon fade into meaninglessness. One of the effects of journal keeping is that it compels you to reflect on the nature, quality, and purpose of your daily experience. Your journal leaves you with something tangible instead of a blurred impression. You have a record and a heightened recollection to show for the part of your life you just lived.

The process of journal keeping engages both the left and right sides of your brain—the analytical, problem-solving side, and the creative, imaginative side. It can be a record not only of the physical, measurable data of your life—*when, what, where*—but of abstract impressions. It's where you seek the answer to the critical question: *What did it mean?*

Does such attention to your schedule mean you're obsessive-compulsive or self-absorbed? Not at all. What it means is you've taken charge of your time. Which is to say, your life. It means you are on the path to Mastery.

Here are reasons why you should keep a journal:

— *Journal keeping creates a feedback loop with your subconscious.*

Recording your innermost observations connects those thoughts to your subconscious mind, creating a feedback loop by which they stimulate *new* thoughts and fresh solutions.

— *Journal keeping sharpens your focus.*

Fuzzy problems receive clarity when you've described them in your journal. You have the opportunity to step back and be an observer of your activities. You can better identify the trivialities that consume undue attention in your life and help you focus on what's important.

— *Journal keeping (and your WIWTH list) permits you to visualize outcomes.*

With your objectives clearly imagined and recorded in your journal, you can form an action plan for accomplishing them. You move from having vague and unclear objectives to visualizing *exactly* the outcome you desire.

— *Journal keeping is a way of logging the progress of your mission.*

Think of your journal as the equivalent of a ship's log, a daily record of a voyage. Some of the entries will be mundane, some will be momentous. If you veer off course in the progress of your mission, you'll have a record of what you did wrong. If you score a huge success, you'll know what you did right.

— *Your journal is the accounting ledger for your most valuable asset.*

As you draw from the balance of your time account, your journal is a record of expenditures. At frequent intervals you can reflect on the value of each withdrawal. *Why did I do that? Was it worth it? Would I do it again?*

— *Journal keeping is personal.*

Your journal is where you have a conversation with yourself. You can discuss problems and choices that you may not want to relate to anyone else. You can address yourself, a third party, or a higher being. It's *your* record. You can be as frank or as blunt as you wish. The knowledge that your journal is for you alone becomes liberating. As you grow more comfortable with the journal, your writing will become spontaneous and creative.

— *Your journal is a repository of ideas.*

This is where you store that great novel idea, the dream you just had, impressions received from a new acquaintance, a quote you don't want to forget. Sketch scenes and maps. Tape clippings, photos, letters in your notebook. If necessary, attach a closeable folder inside the cover.

— *Journal keeping is good for your health.*

Your journal serves as an outlet for pent-up emotions. Numerous studies show that writing down feelings that have been bottled up inside you allows you to let them go. Your physical and mental health receives a boost and you experience an improved sense of well being.[1]

Art Journaling

Painting is just another way of keeping a diary.
—PABLO PICASSO

A variation of the handwritten journal is art journaling. While written journal entries record the measurable data of your life, art journaling is a way of capturing your more abstract thoughts.

Adding visual impressions to your written journal produces a synergy of your most creative skills.

Art? But what if you're not an artist?

Not a requirement. Just as writing is thinking, so is art. Sketching in your journal can bring coherence to your writing. New ideas will present themselves. Solutions to problems may come swimming to the surface from your journal pages. Making visual impressions of your experiences is a way of locking them into memory.

What to draw? Let your imagination roam. Assign smiley or frowning faces as appropriate to people and scenes. Use symbols, shapes, stick figures. Draw maps of your wanderings. Try different colored pens. Draw buildings, airplanes, mountains, animals you encounter.

Even if you don't consider yourself a visual person, you'll discover your hand-eye skills improving with practice. Remember that your journal is for an audience of one: *you*. Render your journal art the way children go about coloring or painting—without caring about the results or whether it meets anyone's approval. No rules. No inhibitions. You don't have to stay inside the lines.

When to Write in Your Journal

The palest ink is stronger than the most miraculous memory.
—CHINESE PROVERB

Any moment when you can pause to reflect on the events of your day is a good time. An especially good time is at the end of your day while the happenings, good and bad, are fresh in your mind. Writing them down, applying a meaning to your experience, has the effect of expunging them from your consciousness. It allows you to go to bed without the monkey chatter of unprocessed thoughts keeping you awake.

Another useful time is first thing in the morning. This kind of journaling has a different slant and purpose than the normal recording of daily events. Called "morning pages," they can be a separate notebook. In her book *The Artist's Way,* Author Julie Cameron calls this mode of journaling "spiritual windshield wipers."[2]

Morning pages are a way of trapping those elusive flashes of creativity that flit across your mind in the early hours when your day still lies unfolded before you. Again, it is recommended that you do this in longhand because your entries can better flow from a stream of consciousness. No rules, no editing, no censors. Let the ideas, complaints, aspirations, frustrations, expectations flow unimpeded onto the page.

Morning pages perform a companion task to night journaling. Instead of purging your mind of the collected thoughts of the day, you are capturing new ideas on paper so that you begin your day with a fresh burst of creativity.

<> <> <>

Profiles in Mastery

Story Musgrave

Whap. Thunk. Smack.

Cyprus limbs and palm fronds slap the cab of the old army surplus truck. Motoring through the sinkholes and swamps of his Florida farm, the grinning driver in the faded khakis and droopy hat has the appearance of a man on a mission.

And he is. Several missions, in fact.

Dr. Story Musgrave pursues missions, adds credentials, collects skills like most people acquire clothes. As a self-taught arborist, he cultivates some forty-five different species of palm tree on his farm. A collector of old machinery, he tends and tweaks each of the rare tractors, trucks, and autos in his barn. As a poet-philosopher, Musgrave writes with spellbinding clarity about man's role in the cosmos.

And more. It was this same Story Musgrave who, clad in a white space suit and suspended 368 miles above the earth, performed the critical repairs on the orbiting Hubble telescope. During the astronaut-surgeon's thirty years with NASA, he logged six Shuttle missions and over 1200 hours in space.

Story Musgrave's journey to Mastery had an unlikely beginning. A high school dropout, he was hitchhiking around the country when he decided to join the Marine Corps in 1953. He left the military with an equivalency diploma and entered Syracuse University in New York. It was the beginning of an academic odyssey.

After completing a BS in math in two-and-a-half years, Musgrave tacked on an MBA, then worked at the Eastman company in operations research until his interest in the human brain led him back to school. He earned a pre-med degree in chemistry, then went to Columbia for an MD in 1964. While at the University of Kentucky for surgical internship, he managed to add masters degrees in physiology and biophysics.

And, in his spare time, he learned to fly. He earned instructor and air transport ratings, flying charters on weekends, all while he was still in internship and grad school. As if that weren't enough, he took up skydiving, logging nearly 800 jumps in order to study the ballistics of the human body.

One day during this period Musgrave read something that struck him like a thunderbolt. NASA was selecting a new group of astronauts with scientific backgrounds. Musgrave applied. Of the thousands of applicants, he and ten others made the cut.

"We were going to the moon," Musgrave remembers, "and we were going incredibly fast." And not just the moon. Musgrave had no doubt that he would be on his way to Mars.

NASA: Story Musgrave

His first year with NASA was spent in Air Force flight training, from which he graduated at the top of his class. But fifteen more years would pass before Musgrave would go into space—not to Mars but into low earth orbit aboard the Space Shuttle Challenger. Meanwhile he pursued new missions. While at the Space Center, he moonlighted as a trauma surgeon at the Denver General Hospital. He served as a part time professor at the University of Kentucky Medical Center. He flew NASA's T-38 Talon trainers, racking up more flight time in the sleek jet than anyone in the world. In his spare time he took courses at the University of Houston, adding yet another master's degree, this one in literature, to his collection. A NASA manager joked, "Musgrave has more degrees than a thermometer."

When Musgrave flew his sixth and last Shuttle mission in December 1996, he was sixty-one, then the oldest human to fly in space. With the possibility of future missions near zero, he hung up his space suit. It was time for new missions.

He became a farmer. And a tree surgeon. And a poet. And a globe-circling speaker and consultant. And a professor. And a husband for the third time, a father for the seventh time.

In his eighties, Musgrave has no intention of slowing down. "Yeah," he says, "I guess I burn the candle at three ends. But if you have a reason to live, you're going to live longer. You just get up in the morning, and you go out and grab life."

Yellow Padding

Where does inspiration come from? From what source do you find solutions to problems? How can you summon ideas from within your subconscious? How do you free your imagination when it becomes stuck?

Here's one answer. It's a technique called yellow padding, so named because of the yellow ruled legal pad used in this example. Yellow padding is another form of thinking by writing. When problems defy solution and ideas refuse to flow, the blank, ruled page of a writing pad can be your window to clarity. For this purpose any writing surface will do—sketching tablet, scratch pad, stationery, even a digital device—but the low-tech blank page of the legal pad is an ideal tool to facilitate the flow of ideas between your eyes and your hand and your brain.

Yellow padding is a version of the psychoanalytical technique called free association developed by Sigmund Freud as an alternative to hypnosis for his subjects. Freud wrote, "We instruct the patient to put himself into a state of quiet, unreflecting self-observation, and to report to us whatever internal observations he is able to make—taking care not to exclude any of them, whether on the ground that it is too disagreeable or too indiscreet to say, or that it is too unimportant or irrelevant, or that it is nonsensical and need not be said."[3]

Just as writing in your journal provides focus on your daily activities, jotting thoughts on a blank yellow pad opens channels to the creative side of your brain. The critical difference between journal keeping and yellow padding is that the yellow pad is temporary. Nothing you write on the pad need be saved—nothing except those magic moments that emerge like gold nuggets from the free-flowing stream of your imagination.

Yellow padding is best done in a venue separate from your usual work station. Find a quiet place—garden, patio, library—and relax. Let your eyes focus softly on a distant object. Mentally distance yourself from the workaday issues that clutter your mind.

The only rule in yellow padding is that there *are* no rules. Nothing is off limits. Spelling, grammar, coherence—none of that counts. No editing is required. What you write is a throwaway document for your eyes only. Nothing is too wacky, absurd, beyond the pale. Your yellow pad jottings can be an outpouring of anger, a confessional, or something genuinely profound. Let it flow. When the page is full, flip the page. Don't stop. Keep it flowing.

The applications of yellow padding are endless. Perhaps you're stuck trying to come up with a marketing strategy for your new product. Or you've reached an impasse in your effort to learn French. Or the plot of your unfinished novel has hit a road block. No matter how hard you try, nothing comes to mind. Your brain keeps recycling the same old ideas you've tried and discarded in the past.

Yellow pad time. Push away from the desk and keyboard. Withdraw to your quiet place, relax, enter a meditative state. Begin writing.

It doesn't matter where you start. Let an idea—any idea—flow onto the page, then follow it as if it were a meandering butterfly. Use arrows, balloons, symbols—any form of written or graphic expression that depicts your thoughts. If an idea connects to another idea, fine. If it lies inert on the page, leading nowhere, that's fine too.

Be curious. Ask questions. Where did that thought come from? How does that idea relate to the previous idea? How far can you take it before it morphs into something else? What does the idea *look* like? Can you sketch it on your pad?

Remind yourself that you're not creating content for an audience. *You* are the audience. You are the conduit for the transfer of thoughts from your subconscious mind to the writing surface. The process may be seen as a form of directed daydreaming, allowing submerged ideas to pop to the surface like gifts from the sea.

Will the solution to your problem always present itself? Of course not. Sometimes the answer must be teased out over time. Sometimes after numerous unproductive yellow padding sessions, the solution will appear at an unlikely moment—during a walk, a dream, an unrelated conversation.

Sometimes the miraculous happens. After being stymied by your unsolvable problem, you are struck with an altogether different—and better—course of action. And where did the solution come from? From the source of all breakthrough solutions: the limitless bounty of your own imagination.

---

[1]   In an article entitled "Emotional And Physical Health Benefits Of Expressive Writing," Authors Karen Baikie and Kay Wilhelm report that "Over the past 20 years, a growing body of literature has demonstrated the beneficial effects that writing about traumatic or stressful events has on physical and emotional health." http://apt.rcpsych.org/cgi/content/full/11/5/338

[2]   Julia Cameron, author of *The Artist's Way*, offers a companion book, *The Artist's Way Morning Pages Journal*. The journal pages are accompanied by passages from *The Artist's Way* and lots of advice on how to use these morning musings as a jumpstart tool for creativity. Says Cameron, "Once we get those muddy, maddening, confusing thoughts [nebulous worries, jitters, and preoccupations] on the page, we face our day with clearer eyes."

[3]   Sigmund Freud, *Introductory Lectures on Psycho-Analysis* (PFL 1) p. 328

Part Two

Getting Physical

It is exercise alone that supports the spirits, and keeps the mind in vigor.
— MARCUS TULLIUS CICERO

ROBERT GANDT AND GARY A. SCOTT

6

The Fitness Mission

We do not stop exercising because we grow old; we grow old because we stop exercising.
   —DR. KENNETH COOPER, author of *Aerobics*

Charlie Futrell smiled at the applause as he sprinted across the finish line. He was used to it. The crowds always gave Charlie a big hand even when he wasn't the winner. The actual winner of the Central Florida triathlon crossed the line long ago, but Charlie was still the crowd's favorite. He would have been the winner in his age class—if there were such a class. He was the only competitor in the over-ninety group.

A triathlon was no big deal for Charlie Futrell. This was his 119th such event, including four Ironman competitions in Hawaii. Charlie was a classic.[1] And so are you.

All classic machines—cars, airplanes, people—deteriorate from disuse. Museum pieces may look good, but they're functionless. To maintain peak performance, your body and brain demand exercise. And like all classic machines, they require regular maintenance.

Which means that when something breaks, you have it fixed. When a part wears out, you have it replaced. If it's an irreplaceable part, you find a workaround. Whatever it takes, you keep the machine running. You are the owner—and maintainer—of your classic body and brain. The old cliché *use it or lose it* has never been more screamingly true.

Your body is a metaphor for your personal universe. In no other realm of your existence do you have such singular control. The rest of your universe—family, career, relationships, the economy, the environment, politics—all can change or be taken

53

from you despite your best efforts. Your interaction with them requires mutual cooperation, consent, compromise.

But there are two aspects of your life over which you have exclusive jurisdiction—your mind and your body. What you eat, how you exercise, how you think—these are yours alone to manage.

Mastery is about taking control of those aspects.

Your overall fitness—physical and mental—is the sum total of how you think, work, sleep, eat, exercise, and feel about yourself. Every mission in your pursuit of Mastery demands both physical and mental vigor. Only by being fit will you have the energy, stamina, and clarity to fulfill your missions. Fitness then should be viewed not just as an objective but as a requisite condition.

Fine, you say, but *what* is fitness? How is fitness determined? Is there some level at which you thump your chest and declare yourself physically fit? Most important, what does it take to *become* fit versus *staying* fit?

The short answer: it takes a mission.

Fitness: Where to Begin

Most of us think we don't have enough time to exercise. What a distorted paradigm! We don't have time not to.
—STEPHEN COVEY

Getting in shape . . . You've heard the term all your life. And it seems like a worthy goal: being fit, healthy, in good condition. What's wrong with that?

Nothing. Nothing except that "getting in shape" is too fuzzy a goal for your purposes. Simply being fit, by whatever definition, lacks specificity. How fit is fit? Fit for what? More or less fit than whom? Worse, it usually has no timeline or measurable objective—key components of any mission of Mastery.

You can spend much of your life flailing at fitness activities—health club memberships, sporadic jogging, biking, doing the at-home exercise-du jour you saw on television. The results are murky and immeasurable. Maybe you feel more fit, but you're not sure why. Maybe you gained strength, but how much?

Dutifully putting in the miles or reps or laps, month after month, all in the name of fitness, becomes. . . sorry to say, boring. And unrewarding. Yes, you may notice over time an extra layering of muscle, a faster lap time, more pounds on the weight bar.

Or you may not.

The results depend on your motivation, which usually wanes after the first leveling off in performance. With no discernable progress, fitness regimens become tedious.

What's missing is a mission.

Here's how to convert that dreamy *I'll get in shape someday* aspiration to a mission. Begin by applying the principles of Mastery:

— **Define the objective.**

Make it specific. If you're a runner, it can be a target of a six, ten, twelve minute or more mile. It doesn't matter as long as you set the bar somewhere beyond your current level. Or make it a singular accomplishment such as climbing Mt. Kilimanjaro or trekking the Appalachian Trail that demands a specific fitness level. Or make it the completion of a challenging event such as a road race, triathlon, a long distance bike rally, an open ocean swim event.

— **Make the goal attainable.**

Be realistic. Setting the bar too high can produce discouragement and loss of confidence. The objective must be within an acceptable challenge/skill ratio. Not too easy, not so beyond your current level that success seems impossible. Steve Kotler, in *The Rise of Superman*, defines the sweet spot as the thin zone where the challenge exceeds your current capability by 4%. That may seem a hard-to-measure value, but the concept is valid.

— Apply a time frame.

Training for a scheduled event like a 10K run or bike race has the built-in benefit of a target date. The phases of your training program will be sequenced to culminate on the target date. If your goal is something more self-directed such as a personal best performance, set your own target date and schedule the steps you must take to attain the goal. *You* are in control.

— Make a Mission Plan.

This is integral to all pursuits of Mastery. Your mission plan contains your objective, your schedule, and all pertinent observations about the mission. Use the same document to record your progress. Only by measuring your advancement can you realize the true success of the mission.

And of course . . .

— Commit.

The Big C. One immediate benefit of selecting an organized event is that you have to *sign up*. Sometimes it is the very act of declaring your intention in writing—*I'm gonna do it*—and perhaps plunking down an entry fee that transforms a vague aspiration into a commitment. If your mission is aimed at a singular achievement—a specific level of performance or a physical accomplishment—then plainly state your intention in your mission plan.

[1] Charlie Futrell passed away on August 21, 2012 at the age of ninety-two. "He was definitely an inspiration for all the younger athletes," said Fred Sommer, owner of Sommer Sports in Clermont in the *Orlando Sentinel*. "It's probably what helped him to live longer. The drive to keep training . . . he was always a special part of the race."

7

Hit the Road

Me thinks that the moment my legs begin to move, my thoughts begin to flow.
—HENRY DAVID THOREAU

You were born to walk, hike, run. You are a superbly evolved bipedal animal with an elegant linking of tendons, muscles and body structure that allow you to transit the planet with greater efficiency than almost any other species of mammal. Your innate ability to hit the road on your feet is not only a gift, it is essential to your physical well-being. And yet . . .

This natural gift has been allowed to atrophy in a vast number of senior adults. The sad truth is that most can endure little more that short, brisk walks, and they are paying a severe price in their overall health.

The ability to walk efficiently opens a myriad of pathways in your quest for Mastery. There is no better way to experience a new environment—foreign city, scenic vista, meandering trail—than on foot. Hiking on picturesque ranges and plateaus provides an almost mystical mind-body-earth connection that merges your consciousness with nature.

One of the greatest benefits to be derived from walking is to your health. A daily program of moderate-intensity walking can:

— *Reduce the risk of coronary heart disease*

— *Reduce the risk of non-insulin dependent (type 2) diabetes*

— *Help maintain a healthy weight*

— *Lessen the chances of osteoporosis*

— *Lower blood pressure and blood sugar levels*

— *Reduce anxiety, boost your mood*

— *Provide therapy in recovering from illness or injury*

How much walking does it take to achieve these benefits? A commonly used number for how many steps you should walk each day is 10,000. Since the average person's stride is approximately 2.5 feet, 10,000 steps amounts to nearly five miles. In daily life the inactive adult takes 3,000 steps or less. That means taking another 7,000 or so steps in a sustained walk or run.

Fine, you say, but how do you measure 10,000 steps? Easy, at least if you're wearing one of the newer high-tech pedometers that track your steps throughout the day. Choices range from a unit like the Fitbit wristband that counts steps, walking time, distance, and calories burned to a pocket device like the Omron Pocket Pedometer, which tracks your steps and allows you to upload the data to your smartphone or computer.

Does it make a difference how fast you walk? Yes, despite the bogus theory that covering a given distance requires the same energy regardless of the pace. A brisker, more vigorous pace *does* require greater energy and burns significantly more calories. A 160 lb. person walking one mile at a leisurely twenty-minute-per-mile pace burns eighty-five calories. Bumping up the pace to twelve-minutes-per-mile (the break point between speed walking and jogging) burns 116 calories.(3)

And what walking pace is brisk enough to produce results? It depends on the walker's physical condition. For out-of-shape beginners, a 16-to-18-minute per mile pace is enough. "You should be able to converse, but not sing," says Richard Cotton, a spokesman for the American College of Sports Medicine in Indianapolis. "You should feel like if you moved any faster, you'd be breathless."(4) A more accurate way to determine your correct pace is by monitoring heart rate—a technique which we'll explore later.

Walking can be an effective aerobic exercise for almost everyone. You can walk day or night, in almost any weather, any environment, alone or with partners. If you want to stay indoors, you can even accomplish your step-count on a stationary platform (though you'll miss most of the head-clearing benefit of walking in the open spaces). If you have health considerations, weight control problems, walking is an eminently suitable protocol. If you are on a mission of attaining fitness, a structured walking program is a great beginning.

Or perhaps you're ready for something more. If you have already reached a basic plateau of aerobic fitness, consider taking it to the next level.

Running? At My Age?

> *If you run, you are a runner. It doesn't matter how fast or how far. It doesn't matter if today is your first day or if you've been running for twenty years. There is no test to pass, no license to earn, no membership card to get. You just run.*
>
> —JOHN BINGHAM

Few fitness protocols are more basic than running. You can run almost anywhere, in any conditions, with minimal investment in clubs, clothes, or equipment. Running is a superb exercise for weight loss, cardio training, or simply for the mindful, meditative state that a slow, rhythmic pace can induce.

But wait, you say. Is running really a good idea for everyone? Certainly not. Not for those with damaged joints. Not for those with existing cardiovascular disease. Not for anyone with serious health concerns—until they get clearance from their doctor to hit the road in running shoes.

Yes, running comes with risks. And yes, the percentage of runners who incur injuries to feet, knees, hips is significant. Significant enough to imply that running is one of the more dangerous physical activities you can pursue. And yet . . .

There are ways to experience the benefits of running—at any age—without injury and without overstressing your joints or cardiovascular system. But first, let's address some of the truths—and myths—about running. If you are a runner, or you know a runner who has been injured, or you are a runner who has quit running, you've heard them:

— *Running will ruin your knees.*

— *Impact sports (such as running) are bad for your joints.*

— *Humans weren't meant to run long distances.*

— *Taking up running after middle age is dangerous.*

— *The constant impact of running can ruin your eyesight.*
    — *If you run after the age of [fill in the blank—50, 60, beyond] you're likely to have a [fill in the calamity—stroke, heart attack, hernia, crippling joint failure, ad infinitum . . .].*

As with all such warnings, let's separate the truth from the hearsay. Here are some facts about running and its effect on your body.

The cause of most joint problems in senior adults is *not* the cumulative wear and tear from exercise. The culprit behind most joint pain is the invisible enemy—osteoarthritis. And where does osteoarthritis come from? Blame your parents. Or an old injury. Or blame yourself for your previously sedentary lifestyle.

Running may actually improve the symptoms of arthritis. Evidence shows that in the absence of use the articular cartilage—that's the tissue that covers the ends of bones in your joints—degenerates and sets you up for osteoarthritis. There is clear evidence that moderate exercise can actually *improve* the symptoms of arthritis without causing further joint damage.[1] And regarding the notion that running can affect your eyesight—relax.

There is no evidence that running —or any other aerobic exercise— has a negative effect on visual acuity. To the contrary, research shows that strenuous exercise may help prevent vision loss.[2] Age-related problems such as macular degeneration and cataracts have been shown to occur with lesser frequency in men and women with a history of regular running.

Running may actually extend your life. Studies of the associations of premature death with specific exercises show that a program of moderate jogging extended the lives of the study subjects. The key word here is "moderate." The investigators found that between one hour and two-and-a-half hours per week delivered the optimum exercise-vs.-mortality ratio.

Running delivers multiple health benefits. Running at a moderate pace improves oxygen uptake, increases insulin sensitivity, lowers blood pressure, and increases bone density.[3] What pace qualifies as "moderate?" "You should aim to feel a little breathless," advises Dr. Peter Schnohr, chief cardiologist of the Copenhagen City Heart Study, "but not very breathless." (More about breath and heart rate target zones later).

Or . . . you can simply forget all such structured approaches. Consider running for the purest of reasons—to be in the outdoors, alone with your thoughts. You can indulge in the most primal form of the sport, trail running. You are free to run, walk, jog, sprint, lope—all at your own pace, your own distance, tailoring your outing to suit your mission.

You *do* have a mission, right?

How to Run Without Injury

Running is a road to self-awareness and reliance; you can push yourself to extremes and learn the harsh reality of your physical and mental limitations or coast quietly down a solitary path watching the earth spin beneath your feet.

MASTERY

—DORIS BROWN HERITAGE

Some of the warnings about the hazards of running have validity. True, almost all runners, at one time or another, incur temporary injuries. Also true is that almost all these injuries are preventable. Almost all you can recover from and resume running.

Here are some common sense ways to enjoy running *without* incurring an injury.

Listen to your body.

If you sense pain— knee, hip, foot, or any other warning sign—you're receiving a warning from your body. It's a signal to back off. Try to determine what is causing the discomfort. Is it associated with your stride, your shoes, the terrain? Bottom line: If running causes pain, stop and check it out.

Get the right shoes.

There is a non-stop debate about which is better—max-cushion, motion-stabilized road shoes or minimalist footgear that fits your foot more like a glove and approximates barefoot running. Each has its merits, but most runners, especially senior athletes, will find that something in between suits them best. Your choice also depends on whether you run on hard surface, dirt, the beach, or on rocky trails. If you're new to running, or just coming back, get the advice of an experienced shoe fitter at a technical running store. Bring your most worn pair of running or walking shoes to show the wear pattern on the sole.

Get the right size.

Most runners require a running shoe one or two sizes larger than their street shoe. Go by how the shoe feels, not the size on the label. Take your time. If the store won't let you run in the shoe, find another store.

Learn to run without stressing your joints or incurring injury.

If you are just beginning a running program, or returning to running after years away, consider a technique such as the <u>Chiwalk-Run</u> program. Based on the principles of the ancient martial art T'ai Chi, the walk-run technique is a gentle, mindful approach to running. The objective is to reduce impact, stay pain-free, and run with confidence. Technique, more than equipment or running surface, will prevent injury.

Walk, Run, Sprint

I run because if I didn't, I'd be sluggish and glum and spend too much time on the couch. I run to breathe the fresh air. I run to explore. I run to escape the ordinary. I run ... to savor the trip along the way. Life becomes a little more vibrant, a little more intense. I like that.
— DEAN KARNAZES, ultra marathoner

Breaking up your run into segments is an effective way for new and returning runners to ease into the exercise without feeling depleted afterward. By inserting a sprint segment into each session you will be expanding your aerobic envelope. Your running sessions will gradually become easier, more pleasurable.

Here's the drill: Begin your run with a warm up segment of brisk walking. Pay attention to your breathing rate. Notice your heart rate (more about heart rate monitoring coming up). Allow about five minutes of cardio warm up before you begin an easy running pace. Maintain a pace that produces your target heart rate (which you'll soon learn to determine by your breathing rate). Run

66

until you sense tiredness, or your heart rate exceeds the top end of the target zone. Note the time and resume walking for half the amount of time you spent running. This ratio—two-to-one running/walking—is flexible. You'll continue to modify the ratio as your fitness level improves.[4]

When you're fully warmed up—and before you sense tiredness— run for no more than one minute at nearly max pace. This is the sprint segment, an abbreviated form of interval training and is the only portion of the run in which you will elevate your heart rate to anywhere near its maximum. Do this carefully and note the results. If the sprint causes pain or undue fatigue, leave it out of your next sessions. Over time, the sprint intervals will have the effect of gradually expanding your aerobic capability. You may also notice an enhanced energy following your walk-run-sprint session.

Keep modifying your running program to match your progress. As you improve, shift the walk/run ratio to more running and less walking. Keep it conservative.

How will you know how you're doing? The best way (you knew this was coming) is to keep a log. Your running log will include your time/distance, walk/run ratio and—this is important—*how you feel*. Were you fatigued, energized, bored, focused, motivated? Did you experience pain or discomfort? By paying attention to the details of your running sessions, you are more likely to remain motivated to continue the program.

Above all, keep it pleasurable. If hitting the road becomes an unrewarding grind, you're doing it wrong. Remember that your goal is not simply to log miles or hours or pile up statistics. Running, like fitness itself, can be a portal through which you pass on your journey to Mastery.

---

[1] In a *Runner's World* article, November 1, 2001, "Running and the Risk of Osteoarthritis," Benjamin Ebert, M.D., PhD. asks, "What is the risk of osteoarthritis for runners in

particular?" Then Ebert answers his own question: "Several studies provide evidence that runners, even those who have run competitively for many years, do not have an increased prevalence of osteoarthritis."

2   In a controlled study, Dr. Paul Williams, epidemiologist in Berkeley Lab's Life Sciences Division, followed approximately 29,000 male runners and 12,000 female runners for more than seven years. Men who ran more than 5.7 miles per day had a 35 percent lower risk of developing cataracts than men who ran less than 1.4 miles per day. The study also analyzed men's 10-kilometer race performances, which is a good indicator of overall fitness. The fittest men boasted one-half the risk of developing cataracts compared to the least-fit men. A second study found that running appeared to reduce the risk of age-related macular degeneration. In the study, 152 men and women reported being diagnosed with the disease. Compared to people who ran less than 1.2 miles per day, people who averaged between 1.2 and 2.4 miles per day had a 19 percent lower risk for the disease, and people who ran more than 2.4 miles per day had between 42 percent and 54 percent lower risk of the disease.

3   Dr. Peter Schnohr, speaking at the "Assessing prognosis: a glimpse of the future" symposium, declared, "We can say with certainty that regular jogging increases longevity. The good news is that you don't actually need to do that much to reap the benefits."

4   Jeff Galloway, veteran runner and writer, advocates in his book Running Until You're 100 a run/walk ratio tailored to your pace per mile. Faster runners (7:00—9:30 minutes per mile) should run for longer segments, walk shorter. Slower runners (10:00+ per mile) run/walk

nearly equal amounts and in shorter segments. Example: A pace of 13:30 calls for running one minute and walking one minute. "In general," says Galloway, "I've found that older runners benefit more from shorter running segments , with more frequent walk breaks, even when the walks are shorter."

8

The Art of Breathing

When setting a goal, make small goals that will ultimately lead to a large goal. For your large goal, it is also beneficial to have an A and B goal. One might be the "dream goal," a higher or more difficult goal, and the other a more achievable goal.

—SCOTT JUREK, best-selling author and ultra marathoner

Athletes have long talked about "the Zone"—the Zen-like state wherein they feel almost detached from their bodies and they function at peak performance. Reaching the Zone had always seemed an elusive and unrepeatable moment. It happened with magical randomness. The first man to break the four-minute-mile barrier, Roger Bannister, described the experience: "We seemed to be going so slowly. There was no strain. There was no pain. Only a great unity of movement and aim. The world seemed to stand still or even not exist."

What if it were possible to enter the Zone at will? What if, instead of straining your body to exhaustion, you could perform with a seemingly effortless flow? What if you could experience that euphoric sense of detachment whenever you chose? What if in the pursuit of Mastery you could enter the Zone whenever you chose? What if . . .

Perhaps you can. Dr. John Douillard, author of *Body, Mind, and Sport*, believes that you can reach the Zone in sports performance through a mind-body training regimen. The first requirement is to cultivate that delicious feeling of effortlessness experienced in the Zone. Douillard, a former professional athlete and sports medicine practitioner, disdains the conventional "no pain, no gain" philosophy, particularly when applied to senior athletes. The greatest training benefit is derived, he believes, from training at *half* your maximum capacity.

Half? Douillard's premise, not surprisingly, is controversial. Training at something far less than maximum capacity flies in the face of everything generations of trainers have told us. We've always believed that you acquire strength, speed, and endurance only by pushing yourself to your physical limits. Pouring on the coal, stretching your maximum numbers. Which *does* produce results, but perhaps not of the lasting kind. Nor does it produce the state we call the Zone. Ultimately your body and mind will reject the steady regimen of gasping, maxed-out training.

The evidence supports this belief. A study published by long time running guru and father of the aerobics revolution, Dr. Kenneth Cooper, says that for longevity and health, exercise should be done at *less* than 60% capacity.

Fine, but if such a regimen enhances longevity and health, can it also extend the top end of our performance level?

Yes, says Douillard. One of the ways to train at this level is by breathing through the nose. The deep diaphragmatic breathing technique by which we attain the alpha state in meditation can produce a similarly calming effect in sports. The objective of deep nasal breathing is to produce the same oxygen flow at a lower heart rate and, thus, a lower perceived exertion.

Watch athletes in motion. Most, you will observe, are breathing through their mouths during high exertion. At any fitness center or road race you'll see contorted faces, mouths agape, looking as if they're in extreme discomfort. And they are. They're in oxygen debt.

From an early age you've been conditioned to switch to mouth breathing at the first sign of stress. It's a survival instinct, your source of emergency oxygen. Mouth breathing is associated with the fight-or-flight impulse, which automatically accelerates the heart rate and produces a high stress level. This served your ancestors well when they were running from saber-toothed tigers.

It doesn't serve you well in your pursuit of optimal, effortless performance.

For exercise to fulfill the goals of your mission, it must have a lasting effect. You're not shooting for a gut-busting, one-shot performance so that you can check off another bucket list item. You're seeking an advanced state of training that will deliver the euphoric experience of the Zone. Your goal is a training regimen that will prepare you to stretch your boundaries, to realize your fullest potential. To fulfill your mission.

Nasal Breathing for Reducing Stress

An ancient nasal breathing exercise called *ujayi pranayama* is known to produce a deep relaxing effect. A similar method is advocated by John Douillard both for exercise and relaxation. He calls it Darth Vader breathing, and as soon as you've tried it, you'll see why. Here's how to do it:

1. **In a relaxed state, inhale and exhale normally through the nose.**

2. **As you exhale, constrict your throat and make a slight snoring sound.** The feeling you get in your upper throat is that air is *not* passing out your nostrils. It is. There's no other way out.

3. **During the exhale, while making the snoring sound, notice that your abdominal muscles are slightly contracting.** They *have* to contract in order to produce the sound. The tighter you make your stomach muscles, the more resonant (and scary) the sound will be.

4. **When you've got the soft snoring sound right, take it to the next level.** Take deeper inhalations, sucking in as

much air as possible, then squeeze it all out with a conscious abdominal contraction. This will produce the full and eerie Darth Vader sound. Practice the technique, taking maximum breaths while walking or just sitting at your desk. Ignore the curious looks you get.

Taking it on the Road

The next step is to implement nasal breathing in your training. We'll assume you're training for a run, but the same method applies to other disciplines, including weight training, biking, even swimming (yes, believe it or not). Here are the steps in sequence:

— **Before your training session, do some gentle stretching.** Your purpose is to prepare not just your body but your mind for the coming exercise. Yoga is the perfect method for this phase, integrating the mind with the body. Any stretching exercise will do the job as long as it eases you into a relaxed but flexible condition. During your stretching you will use the nasal breathing technique, preparing you for the experience of the Zone.

— **With the mind and body prepared, begin the warm up phase**. This is the brief window during which you exercise mainly the lungs. Run at an easy jog pace—or even a brisk walk. The reason is this: the first rough patch for most runners comes about five minutes into the workout. That's when the breathing rate elevates, and so does the heart rate. If they've gone out at strong enough pace, they may reach an early anaerobic level, going into oxygen debt. Many hardball runners see this as just part of the territory. An early wall they have to power through until they're warmed up. But, as we'll see, there's a better way.

— **While in the warm up phase of the run, continue using deep nasal breathing.** The idea is to fill all the lobes of the lungs, saturating the blood with oxygen. During this warm up you are simulating the effortless, floating sensation you want to experience in the vigorous stage to come. You're prepping your body to perform at a higher level using lower breath and heart rates than you previously required.

— **Gradually pick up the pace.** You're experimenting. Listen to your body. Try to sense the point at which your breathing and heart rates accelerate into the discomfort zone. This should happen somewhere around 50% of your MHR (maximum heart rate).[1] At this point back off, slacken your pace to keep your breathing and heart rate at this level. Continue the run at this pace, nudging it up, slacking back. Try to *feel* the exertion level required to maintain this pace. Do an entire run this way, trying to maintain the same breathing and heart rates.

— **Continue this routine.** With practice you'll discover that nasal breathing comes easier, more naturally. Your breathing rate for any given heart rate will be lower. When the 50% level becomes thoroughly comfortable, try notching it up to 60%. Do you still have the effortless feeling? If so, then your optimum training zone will be between the 50% and 60% marks. After you've become comfortable at this level, you'll probably want to elevate the rate. In the next section we'll show you how to more accurately calculate your target numbers.

Is this the most efficient way to train? Not at all, at least in terms of producing the quickest results. The traditional high-stress aerobic levels of 70 to 90% of maximum exertion will deliver more immediate gains—and exhaustion. For the senior athlete and seeker of Mastery, the lower exertion rate delivers a longer-lasting and more satisfying level of fitness. This technique will enable you to *enjoy* training and prepare you to reach your full potential— *without* injury or losing your motivation.

Remember that one of your goals is to be in the Zone. Train within these parameters and it is likely that you *will* experience that euphoric, effortless feeling. Once there, you'll be hooked.[2]

Target Heart And Breathing Rates

For an accurate assessment of exertion during your training session, you need an HRM—heart rate monitor. The leading brands include Garmin, Polar, Suunto and Timex. HRMs all work by reading electrical signals from your heart and displaying them on the monitor. The two basic types are the finger sensor models and the chest strap devices. The finger sensor type comes with only a wrist monitor with a touchpad sensor, which you must press to activate the sensor and get a readout.

Best suited to your purpose is the chest strap model, which displays constant heart rate data and requires other inputs from you. The basic types give you continuous heart rate data and most models provide average, high, and low numbers. The more advanced (and expensive) models from Suunto and Garmin deliver speed, distance, location via built-in GPS transmitters. Other models come with a shoelace-mounted foot pod that provides distance and pace information almost as accurately as a GPS. The transmitters in some of the higher end units also send encrypted transmissions from the chest strap to the monitor, which prevents crosstalk from your running or biking companions' devices.

Carrying a smartphone on aerobic outings is a good idea, especially on your road bike and during meandering runs away from home. Not only is the phone an emergency communications device, new apps are available that measure your stride, distance, calorie burn, and times using the GPS feature of the phone. Among these are Runkeeper, Endomondo, Digifit, and the Nike+ Running app. Most of these apps give you audio feedback while you run and will keep you within a selected training range.

To establish your optimum training heart rate (OTR), you first need to determine your MHR (maximum heart rate). There are three methods to find this number.

1. Calculate
2. Supervised test by a physiologist (possibly expensive)
3. Going flat out in an exercise sequence (possibly dangerous and not recommended).

To calculate your MRH, you can use the old formula of 220 minus your age. The trouble with this is that the rate change by age is not linear and could produce an artificially lower number for very fit senior athletes.[3] A more accurate formula, offered in a study published in the journal, *Medicine & Science in Sports & Exercise*, is 206.9 - (0.67 x age).[4]

Don't let the math problem intimidate you. You need do this only once, inserting your own numbers in place of the sixty-year-old athlete in our example, and you'll have your personal training envelope.

Here's the formula:

206.9 − (.67X age 60)=166.7 MHR, which we'll round off to 167, our sixty-year-old subject's maximum heart rate.

Next, determine your RHR (resting heart rate). This number is best taken first thing in the morning when you wake up. Let's assume it is 60.

Now you're ready to find your Optimum Training Rate (OTR). Again, there are several accepted methods, each producing slightly different rates. We'll calculate our 60-year-old athlete's OTR by the most commonly accepted method, the Karvonen formula.[5] Again, plug in your own numbers to define your personal rate.

The Karvonen formula: (MHR-RHR) X % intensity) + RHR= Training Zone

    1. 167 (MRH) -60 (RHR)=107 (This number also defines your HRR — Heart Rate Reserve, used in other formulas)

    2.   107 X 50% (low percentage end of training zone)=53.5+60 (RHR)=113.5 This will be the low end of your training zone.

    3. 107 X 60% (high percentage end)= 64.2+60 (RHR)=124.2 This is the high end of the training zone.

An easy way to calculate your heart rate for each of the five training zones is by plugging your numbers into the Digifit[6] site.

In this example, your training zone (between 50% and 60%) bracket, rounded off, is a heart rate between 114 and 124. Sports physiologists call this Training Zone 1, which is recommended for warm up, recovery, and low-stress aerobic training.[7] This is your target zone while perfecting the nasal breathing technique.

Training Zone 2 (between 60% and 70%), called the endurance zone, is a heart rate of between 124 and 134 and is appropriate for workouts of a greater exertion level. Likewise, Zones 3, 4, and 5 ratchet the heart rates up into the anaerobic levels and may not be suitable for senior athletes.

Do the heart rate numbers seem low to you? They may be, depending on your level of fitness, age, and particular sport. Without undergoing a professional testing, you should listen to your own body to determine whether the numbers for your zone need some fine tuning. You may find that different activities— running, biking, exercise machines—require different parameters.

Your heart rate training zone may be **too low** if:

— You have to slow to a walk to remain in the zone.

— At your slowest jogging or work out exertion level (while warmed up and nasal breathing) you still register above the top (60%) bracket.

Your heart rate training zone may be **too high** if:

— You are walking briskly or slow jogging, nasal breathing, and are still below the zone.

— You're at a medium exertion level, nasal breathing at near max, and haven't hit the top end (60%) of the zone.

In these instances, experiment with the training zone boundaries. Tweak them so that your breathing rate and heart rate match your perceived level of exertion. By training within the optimum zone, practicing deep rhythmic nasal breathing, you will gradually see your pace increase while your breathing and heart rates remain at a constant level. When you need to notch it up—a speed trial, group run, or a competition—you'll have built the aerobic reserves to do it.

As you become comfortable with the nasal breathing technique, experiment with patterns of breathing. During this phase it's best *not* to listen to music or audio books or fitness feedback through ear plugs. You want to be free of distractions. Focus totally on the feedback from your body, your breath and heart rates, your perceived level of exertion.

Running by the Numbers

Take a moment to observe other runners on the road and trails. You'll see most—elite athletes as well as plodders—wearing the "runner's mask"—face contorted, mouth open, breathing at a rate of about forty-five breaths a minute (inhalation for two steps, exhalation for two steps at 180 steps per minute).

You're going to do it differently. By breathing through your nose, staying within your training zone, you'll find that you can reduce the number of breaths per minute by half or more. Fewer breaths mean fewer heartbeats, which translates to more efficiency and greater endurance.

If you've given yourself the mission of reaching a specific running goal, this is your ticket to success.

Begin the process by settling into an easy running (or biking, walking, or treadmill) pace. Check your breathing rate. Assuming you're on a run and warmed up, not pushing hard but moving at a comfortable pace, notice how your breath matches your steps. Your inhalation will probably last about four steps. Same for the exhalation. If your running pace is 160 steps per minute, that equates to 20 breaths (inhalation+exhalation) a minute. Pay attention to this rhythm. With practice, you will use this breathing-by-step count as a biofeedback signal. You'll *know* your heart rate and level of exertion without having to look at the heart rate monitor. Even better, you'll be tapping into an ancient source of calm and meditation by focusing your attention on breathing.

When the 4-4 rhythm—four steps each inhalation, four each exhalation— becomes a comfortable rate for you, stay with it for several runs while you experience being in tune with your body. Notice how changing the pace, or running up and downhill affects your breathing. Greater exertion may shorten the rhythm to 3-3. When you're ready, try slowing the breathing rate to 5-5. Or use, as many runners do, a different count for inhalations than exhalations, such as 4-3, or 5-4. See how it affects your pace. This is the time to experiment.

Scott Jurek, renowned ultra marathoner, is a nasal breathing advocate (as well as a believer in training exclusively on a plant-based diet). In his book *Eat & Run*, he acknowledges learning the technique from Douillard's *Body, Mind, and Sport.* Douillard likens performing within the Zone to dwelling in the eye of a hurricane. You are in a place of calm, surrounded by the storms and swirling winds.

It's an apt metaphor not just for aerobic training but for every mission you undertake.

---

1 Douillard, John, *Body, Mind, and Sport* (New York: Three Rivers Press, 2001)

2 The value of nasal breathing in aerobic training is not unanimously agreed upon by experts. An 11 September 2012 article in *Outsideonline.com* quotes Dr. James Saffrath, a physiology lecturer at the University of California, Davis: "Humans deepen each breath when they exercise—it's what we do to increase our oxygen uptake. ... Nose vs. mouth? Doesn't matter." What matters, in the opinions of John Douillard and champion ultra marathoner Scott Jurek, is the effect produced by nasal breathing—a calm, controlled feeling that leads to more efficient running (or any other workout).

3 An alternative—and more stressful—method of determining maximum would be on a controlled exercise, carefully monitoring your heart rate as you reach maximum exertion.

4 Jackson, Andrew S. Estimating Maximum Heart Rate From Age: Is It a Linear Relationship? Med Sci Sports Exerc. 39(5):821, May 2007.

5 Martti Karvonen, developer of the Karvonen formula, was a Finnish physiologist and pioneer in the study of cardiovascular disease epidemiology. J. A. Zoladz is a noted Polish exercise physiologist whose formula for determining any of the five training zone heart rates is somewhat but less precise. For Zone 1 (the optimum

training zone for us): MRH – 50 bpm (beats per minute). The 60-year-old with the MRH of 167 would thus have a target OTR of 117. Zoladz brackets the zone plus or minus 5 bpm, so our athlete's training zone is between 112 and 122, very close to the Karvonen bracket of 114 to 124.

6 In the Digifit grid http://www.digifit.com/heartratezones/training-zones.asp, you can plug in your own numbers and come up with target heart rates, using three different formulae, for each of the HRT training zones (see next note).

7 The heart rate training zones are generally classified like this:
Zone 1 — Warm up, recovery, and low-stress training.
Zone 2 — Endurance
Zone 3 — Stamina
Zone 4 — Economy (anaerobic)
Zone 5 — Speed (anaerobic)
Zone 6 — Max Heart Rate

9

Get it Wet

The water is your friend. You don't have to fight with water, just share the same spirit as the water, and it will help you move.
—ALEKSANDR POPOV, Russian Olympic four-time gold medalist

With aging comes evolving reality. Your body may have reached a point, after sufficient wear and tear, that you can't run. Or hike long distances. Or hoist weights. Or engage in sports that impact your joints.

But there is still an aerobic activity you can perform for virtually the rest of your life. Of all possible fitness missions, few deliver the same payoff as swimming: cardio workout, exercise of almost every muscle group, a mental engagement that allows you to dream and meditate. Swimming provides the same aerobic benefits without the risks to your joints. In fact, swimming is an especially suitable sport for those with arthritic joints and restricted movement.

Swimming is the Zen of aerobic activity. Something magical happens when you enter the water. You defy gravity. You glide like a gull through a silent medium, shedding most of the aches and impediments that hinder you on solid earth. You become one with the water, a creature as fish-like as you are mammal.

"Swimming forces you to focus and sets the mood to meditate," says broadcast journalist and swimming devotee Lyn Sherr. "It allows you to dream big dreams."[1]

The ability to swim does not come naturally. Unlike the primordial skills of walking and running, swimming must be learned. You learn it first for survival, to protect you from drowning. The English poet, Percy Bysshe Shelley, was said to have asked one day, "Why can't I swim? It seems so very easy." To which his friend and biographer, Edward John Trelawny, said, "Because you think you can't." This made sense to Shelley, so he jumped into the Arno River in Italy.

It was bad advice. Shelley sank like a stone. His friend Trelawney had to save him from drowning.[2]

In the beginning you learn to swim for survival. Then you learn for speed and efficiency. The most fortunate are those who have taken it to the next level. They are the ones who swim obsessively, lap after lap, or for the more obsessed, mile after mile in pools, ponds, lakes, open ocean.

They are a small group, but they have made a large discovery. Swimming isn't just fun. It's addictive. Swimming delivers rewards both physical and mental. Hence the question: if swimming is such an ideal physical activity, why aren't more people doing it?

Part of the answer is culture. Swimming was long viewed in America as an elitist sport, favored by a privileged class who could afford pools and private schools. Even when the sport became accessible to the masses, those who didn't learn to swim well when they were young never improved. In their adulthood they believe that it's too late. Too difficult. Too boring.

They're wrong. Just as most adults are wrong about their ability to learn foreign languages and musical instruments, they're dead wrong about swimming.

Learning to swim well—meaning with endurance and effortlessness—is an attainable goal at any age. New techniques, improved knowledge, and the expanding access to community and club pools make swimming a suitable sport for everyone. And in almost no other activity can you progress from ineptitude to competence in so short a time.

There is no single best way to swim, nor a best way to learn to swim. But success comes quicker for almost everyone if they have instruction. The freestyle—in the past called the crawl—is the favored stroke by most lap swimmers, distance swimmers, and triathletes. It is also one of the most subtly complex of athletic movements, a choreography of muscle inputs to produce the slickest passage through the water.

And yes, it's possible to learn an efficient freestyle stroke on your own, but it almost always makes more sense to get expert instruction. A good swim coach can save you hours, perhaps years, of unproductive slogging back and forth in the pool.

Mastering the freestyle requires a willingness to learn new techniques and, as with every worthwhile new skill, application. Here are the basics. Once learned, these steps can transform a weak or mediocre swimmer to one who glides through the water with the slipperiness of a fish.

— **Learn to breathe.**

The art of breathing (again) is as vitally important in swimming as in any other aerobic activity. The most common mistake novice swimmers make is to hold their breath between inhalations. This forces you to exhale and inhale all in one rushed effort, quickly producing an out-of-breath feeling caused by CO_2 accumulating in the lungs. To keep a steady, relaxed swim stroke, concentrate on exhaling the whole time your face is in the water. You'll be emitting a constant stream of bubbles until just before you rotate to the inhale position. Holding your breath tenses you up, which hinders your technique as well as making your chest too buoyant, causing your legs to sink in the water. As you become comfortable fully exhaling before the inhale stroke, try advancing to bilateral breathing inhaling on every third stroke, inhaling on alternate sides. Bilateral breathing will keep your swim stroke symmetrical, thus more efficient, by causing you to roll equally to each side with alternating strokes. For most swimmers, bilateral breathing doesn't come naturally. It will require persistence and practice, but it will be worth it.

— Keep your head aligned with your spine.

If anything is guaranteed to slow your progress through the water, it's the tendency to lift your head. Like a see-saw, your body tilts when your head goes up, lowering your legs and feet in the water and creating immense drag. Stay horizontal in the water by rotating your head to the side to inhale. Between strokes keep your gaze on the bottom of the pool directly beneath you. Again, this requires conscious effort. Use an outside observer or a video to show you whether your head is, in fact, aligned with your body. Making this small change in style can deliver huge benefits in efficiency. Translation: you will swim further, at greater speed, on the same amount of expended energy.

— Rotate your body from one side to the other.

This is fundamental in freestyle swimming. Instead of swimming on your stomach, you alternate sides with each stroke. Rotating to the side produces the most streamlined profile for propelling your body through the water. The rolling moment transfers power to the propulsive arm in the water and adds the strength of your lats, pecs, and core muscles to the stroke. Again, bilateral breathing—inhaling on every third stroke on alternating sides—is a good way to insure rolling enough to either side.

— Kick for stability, not propulsion.

The thrust delivered by a freestyler's flutter kick is a tiny fraction of that delivered by the upper body. Though your legs are the strongest muscles in your body, they are relatively useless for driving you through the water. Conclusion: unless you're training for sprints, you're better off *not* expending precious energy on the inefficient kick. Instead, use a shallow flutter kick with the ankles fully extended to drive the hip to the side for the coming power stroke. An easy flutter kick also has the effect of keeping your feet and legs high in the water, making your body more streamlined.

— Lengthen your stroke.

By rotating well to the side on each stroke, you are able to reach further forward, lengthening your stroke. Visualize reaching *slowly* for the far wall of the pool with your extended hand. This translates to further travel from each stroke, taking fewer strokes for any given distance. Fewer strokes+greater distance=swim longer and faster with less effort.

— Sweeten your "catch and pull."

A good "catch"—the way your hand enters and grasps the water prior to the propulsion stroke—lets you lock on to the water and "pull" it back behind you. If you extend your hand level with your head and then pull, the initial force from your palm is *down*, producing little forward thrust but *raising your upper body*. Your legs descend and you become an unstreamlined barge. The best way: when you extend your leading hand before the next stroke, **slide your hand into the water on a *downward* slant**. Keep your hand and arm well below your head. Your catch and pull will force water mostly *behind* you. And while you're extending your hand, the pressure of the water on the upper side of your hand and arm will *raise* your legs, giving you the sensation of swimming *downhill*—an effect similar to that of a runner's forward lean. Congratulations. You have just become a fish-like aquatic creature.

— Swap hands.

Watch a novice swimmer free styling across the pool. What you see probably resembles a paddlewheel boat, one arm after the other thrashing the water. Here's a technique that will add a new fluidity to your freestyle stroke. If you're already lengthening your body by rotating to each side and reaching for the far wall, you need only wait just a bit longer in the hand-extended glide position before beginning the stroke. Wait until the recovering hand has almost joined the extended hand in the forward glide position. Again, this will take a bit of practice before it begins to seem natural. When you've acquired this new timing—stroke, glide, wait for the recovering hand to join the leading hand, stroke—it will feel like an exhilarating new dance step.

Where to begin? Good instruction will save you hundreds of hours of fruitless drills and lap-swimming. Be sure the coach understands *your* intended mission and tailors his instruction accordingly. Like most subtly complex athletic movements, a good swimming style is easier to *show* than to describe in words.

Several good coaching courses are available on line and on DVD. One of the best is the _Total Immersion_ course administered by swim guru Terry Laughlin. The TI method is described in Laughlin's book, *Total Immersion: The Revolutionary Way to Swim Better, Faster, and Easier*, and in his series of accompanying DVDs. Another variation on the same theme is a course from the U. K. called _SwimSmooth_, which offers DVDs for each level of swimmer—beginner, intermediate, and advanced.

In her book *Swim: Why We Love the Water*, Lynn Sherr quotes Dr. Oliver Sacks, best-selling author, neurologist—and swimmer. At eighty Sacks was still learning, still expanding his range of skills. His swimming milestone: "A longer stroke. And bilateral breathing. For a year it seemed so artificial—now it feels natural."

And what lesson did Sacks, a classic pursuer of Mastery, draw from these efforts? "The plasticity of the human brain. You *can* teach an old dog new tricks. You continue to learn until you die."

As with most missions of Mastery, becoming an accomplished swimmer should be done in the same mindful spirit you apply to learning a martial art, a foreign language, a musical instrument. Study the subject, define your goals, write them down, determine a time frame.

Then, of course, the big ticket item: *commit.*

<> <> <>

Profiles in Mastery

Diana Nyad

Call it obsession. Or, as others have suggested, madness. Diana Nyad called it her Extreme Dream.

Nyad was twenty-eight, at the peak of her physical powers, when she first entered the Caribbean water outside Havana in 1978. Her mission was to swim 103 miles to Key West.

She failed. Blown far off course by heavy winds, headed for Texas instead of Florida, hammered against the sides of her enclosed shark cage, Nyad was removed from the water by her doctors after she'd covered seventy-six miles.

Fast forward thirty-three years to August of 2011. Nyad is back in Havana. "I'm almost sixty-two years old," she told the CNN news crew covering the event, "and I'm standing here at the prime of my life. When one reaches this age, you still have a body that's strong but now you have a better mind."

And then she set out to prove it. She slipped into the water and began swimming toward Florida. Again the elements conspired against her. After twenty-nine hours, far off course and disabled with a severe asthma attack, Nyad conceded defeat.

Failure number two.

But Nyad wasn't finished. Less than two months later she was back in Havana with her support team. On this attempt she managed to cover sixty-seven miles, veering far off to the east. Nearly incapacitated from jellyfish and Portuguese man-of-war stings, she was finally hauled out of the water.

Failure number three.

The next year, in August, 2012, Nyad mounted her fourth campaign to swim from Cuba to Florida. On this attempt she covered more distance than in any of her previous efforts until two successive storms and nine debilitating jellyfish stings finally ended the swim.

Failure number four.

By now Diana Nyad was sixty-three. She didn't need ultra-distance swimming feats to validate her credentials. She was already a world record holder in long distance swimming. Fluent in three languages, the author of three books, co-founder of a successful online fitness business, radio host and television news commentator, sought-after motivational speaker, Diana Nyad was an authentic pursuer of Mastery.

Still, the four failures in the Caribbean were gnawing at her like an old wound. The dream wouldn't go away. A mission unfulfilled. After so many failed attempts, she knew she was labeled by cynics as the crazy woman who kept trying to swim across the Caribbean.

So she kept trying.

On the morning of August 31, 2013, a few days past her sixty-fourth birthday, Nyad was back in Cuba. "This is what I need to remedy my malaise," she told bemused reporters, several of whom had covered the same show before. "I need commitment to take over. That level of commitment has such a high. There is no thinking about regrets or what will I do with the rest of my life. I'm immersed in the everyday, full tilt. It's so energizing."

Again she slipped into the glass-slick water of the yacht harbor outside Havana. Still without a shark cage but protected from jellyfish by a silicone mask, a full bodysuit, gloves and booties, Nyad began the long swim to Florida. She had a new mantra: "Find a way." In the sensory-deprived environment of the Caribbean, as day passed into night and then day again, Nyad repeated her mantra. Find a way.

She did. After fifty-three hours of non-stop swimming, Diana Nyad waded onto the sandy beach at Key West. Dazed and sunburned, face and lips swollen from the anti-jellyfish face mask, she could barely enunciate her words. "Never give up," she told the gathered crowd. "You're never too old to chase your dream."

The effect was mesmerizing. The image of Diana Nyad standing on the Florida shore, mission accomplished, sent a ripple of excitement through a generation of senior Americans. Not only had a woman succeeded in an incredible feat of endurance, it was a woman of their age. Nyad's feat conveyed a powerful message. It meant that they weren't too old to chase their own dreams. They too could find a way.

Learn the Flip Turn

The water doesn't know how old you are.
— DARA TORRES, five-time Olympian who won the last of her twelve medals at the age of forty-one.

So you've acquired a fluid, effortless freestyle stroke. You're doing laps in your club pool, feeling in the Zone, focused on the moment. The water is your friend. What else can you do?

How about a flip turn?

You may be excused for asking *whaaaat?* Isn't a flip turn something Olympic swimmers use to shave microseconds off their times? Something flashy kids and advanced amateurs perform while doing their laps? Doesn't a plain vanilla heads-up flat turn accomplish the same purpose, which is to launch you back in the other direction?

Well, yes. But let's say that you're ready to add a touch of panache to your routine. Or let's say you want to train without indulging in the mini-rest that a flat turn allows you between laps. Or, in the spirit of Mastery, let's just say you're ready to learn something new. You can even be forgiven (or secretly admired, depending on your age) for wanting to insert a cool move into your swimming practice.

Best of all, make it a mission.

The so-called flip turn is actually a half somersault in the water. You perform the maneuver while still an arm's length from the wall of pool, tucking into a ball for the somersault, coming to an inverted position underwater, then kicking off from the wall with the soles of your feet. For a good demo of the technique, check out the article "How to Do a Flip Turn (Freestyle)" in *wikiHow*. Another great visual of the flip turn—as well as many other good visual swimming demos—is from Livestrong.com.

Look disorienting? Not after you'd learned the technique. Get the hang of the somersault by practicing from a standing position in water. It's no different than doing somersaults on the grass when you were a kid. Bend over, tuck your chin to your chest, curl into a ball, and use your gut muscles to pull your body around in a full loop. Remember to exhale through your nose throughout the maneuver or else you'll finish with a snout full of water.

When you can do a complete somersault without becoming disoriented, then practice the same maneuver in mid-pool while you are free styling. After you're comfortable doing somersaults, coming out on the same heading you began, you're ready to take it to the wall.

Let's deconstruct the flip turn to its basic components:

1. **Gauge your distance from the wall.**

    Prepare to execute your somersault when you're about one arm's length from the wall. If your pool is configured with lanes, your lane probably has a black line on the bottom. It's there as a navigational tool. At either end of the black line is a short perpendicular line that makes a T about two feet from the wall. Approaching that Black T is when you begin the flip turn.

2. **Take a last stroke, suck in a breath, and tuck your head.**

Bring both arms to your sides. Tilt your head toward your gut. Tuck your body into a ball. Your butt should come out of the water slightly as you somersault. Remember to breathe out through your nose to avoid filling your nasal cavities with water.

3. Use your hands.

Keep your elbows tucked to your sides, but use your hands to scoop water toward your face. This will help rotate you through the half-somersault.

4. Finish with your back to the bottom of the pool.

As you complete the half somersault, bring your arms over your head and point your hands in the direction you want to be going. At this point you're lying face up to the surface, legs bent.

5. Push off from the wall.

Plant the soles of your feet on the wall, toes straight up. Your head should be about a foot below the surface, your legs bent at a ninety-degree angle. Push off with both feet.

6. Roll over to your stomach.

As you push away from the wall, rotate your body back to the upright position. You can do this easily by just twisting your hands and moving your eyes in the direction you want to rotate. Flutter kick to the surface and begin to pull with the arm that was closest to the bottom of the pool when you rotated.

There. You have all you need to master the flip turn. Is it easy? Not at first. Is it necessary? Of course not. You're simply adding a new skill to your growing repertoire. Consider it a mini-mission on your path to Mastery. As with juggling or no-hands bicycling or balancing on one foot, learning the flip turn requires a certain amount of application. It's worth it.

Remember, Mastery is about experimentation. Try stuff. Evaluate the results. Visualize the desired outcome. And then very soon. . . *caramba!* You'll wonder why it ever seemed difficult.

---

1   In *Swim: Why We Love the Water*, Lynn Sherr rhapsodizes about the role of swimming in her life. "Swimming stretches my body beyond its earthly limits, helping to soothe every ache and caress every muscle. But it's also an inward journey , a time of quiet contemplation , when, encased in an element at once hostile and familiar, I find myself at peace, able—and eager— to flex my mind, imagine new possibilities, to work things out without the startling interruptions of human voice or modern life."

2   Despite his first near-death experience in the water, Percy Bysshe Shelley never learned to swim. The poet eventually drowned at sea.

10

The Strength Mission

Modern bodybuilding is ritual, religion, sport, art, and science, awash in Western chemistry and mathematics. Defying nature, it surpasses it.
—CAMILLE PAGLIA

Few exercise programs produce such quick results as strength training. "Things are probably happening immediately at the cellular level," says Dr. Miriam Nelson, director of the Center for Physical Activity and Attrition at Tufts.[1] In a short time you see and feel the difference. Even joint troubles tend to abate. "In four to six weeks, you might see less pain with arthritis," says Nelson.

Strength training provides a different payback than aerobic exercise. While aerobic activity strengthens the heart and pulmonary system, it doesn't ward off sarcopenia—the gradual loss of muscle mass inherent in aging. A study in Denmark showed that men in their late sixties who'd worked with weights for years had muscle mass similar to men in their twenties. Runners and swimmers of the same age, however, had already experienced significant loss of muscle.[2]

Sarcopenia begins in early adulthood and progresses at a rate of about 7% per decade after age thirty. The process is slow and imperceptible. The end result is the look you associate with the very elderly—a shrunken, frail body, as though part of it were missing.

And part of it *is*. That missing muscle mass is gone. Dematerialized. Gone with it is the elderly person's strength, flexibility, and vital bone density, without which they fall victim to osteoporosis and deadly fractures.

Until only a few years ago it was believed that sarcopenia and its related condition, loss of bone density, was an inevitable fact of aging. Modern science has concluded that this is a bogus belief. One compelling study conducted by Dr. Maria Fiatarone and colleagues at Tufts University in the 1990s focused on ten nursing home residents in Boston. Six women and four men between the ages of eighty-six and ninety-six, all frail and most requiring walkers or canes, undertook a strength building program using machines and free weights.

The results were astonishing. In eight weeks their leg strength tripled. The average size of their thigh muscles increased by more than ten percent. Two of the subjects tossed their canes and began walking unassisted.

So what do we take away from the new evidence about aging? That permanent loss of muscle mass is a choice. That the dematerialized muscle mass and shrunken frame of the elderly are as much a function of lifestyle as of aging. Nowhere is the "use it or lose" axiom more resoundingly vivid.

If you are not actively building muscle, you are shedding it.

But there's a more important conclusion: *the process is reversible*. We now know that you *can* restore muscle mass—at any age.

The need for strength training should be clear. Preserving muscle mass is more than just staying fit or looking good. It affects your ability to withstand disease, survive accidents, and to perform vigorous activities into upper elderhood.

In the elderly, muscle mass can make the difference between an independent existence and assisted living. Many of the infirmities previously blamed on old age are, in fact, a result of losing muscle mass and bone density.

During illness your body burns protein faster than usual, drawing protein components from the muscles. If your protein reserve has already been depleted by loss of muscle mass, you have a reduced ability to fight disease.

Strength training carries with it a transfer effect. As you gain muscular strength you gain the vigor that accompanies it, which transfers to your ability to play sports, perform strenuous activities, enjoy sex. Further, it transfers to the way you feel about yourself. Your attitude becomes more positive. Your confidence grows. Your feeling about yourself is revealed in the way you look.

While men tend to associate more with traditional strength training, the need—and the benefits—may be even more applicable to women. Of the estimated ten million Americans with osteoporosis, eighty percent are women. Estrogen, the vital hormone in women that protects bones, decreases sharply after menopause causing a loss of up to twenty percent of a woman's bone density. The result is that one in two women over fifty will break a bone because of osteoporosis.[3]

The solution? Strength training.

Remember that phenomenon of muscle *and* bone density both dematerializing as you age? Strength training produces an equally phenomenal effect. You can create not only new muscle but *also* new bone.[4] Strength training for women has greater potential to restore bone density than almost any drug regimen—without the side effects.

Strength Training at Any Age

Shutterstock 270754241

What follows are the rudiments of strength training. Our purpose is not to lay out a detailed workout regimen with specific weights or equipment. Nor is it to make you a world class bodybuilder or convert you from a ninety-pound weakling to a sculpted ironman. The objective is to provide an overview of what for you may be an imminently useful mission. In pursuing this mission you not only reverse decades of muscle loss, you gain strength to pursue your other chosen missions.

If you're an experienced iron pumper, feel free to skim past these basic drills. If you're a beginner, regard them not as a guide book but a template from which to construct your own personalized training routine.

The field of strength training includes a myriad of techniques and options. As with all worthwhile missions, you must do your homework. Anyone unfamiliar with weight training would do well to consult a qualified trainer, which every good gym and health club has.

If a picture is worth a thousand words, a video can be worth a million. The internet has become a rich source for how-to videos for almost every specific exercise.

As you explore the arcane world of strength training, you may be overwhelmed by the plethora of different techniques. One thing you will quickly notice: instructors don't all perform an exercise exactly the same way. Again, do your homework. Choose the exercise—and method—that works best for you.

Another thing you'll notice: *everyone* who works out in a gym or health club has an opinion. They'll tell you which exercises you should perform, weights, frequency, and the perfect diet to go with it. Their opinions will range from the absurd to the dangerous.

Listen politely—and tune them out. Such well-intentioned advice will only distract you from your objectives, which are (a) to learn the basics of strength training and (b) construct a personalized training program that is precisely correct for *you*.

Detach yourself from the noise and hubbub of the outside world. Focus on learning the essentials of resistance training. Experiment, measure results, develop the program that best suits your mission. In so doing, you adhere to a cardinal tenet of Mastery: *you* are in control of your body, your mind, your life.

Is it Safe?

If you think lifting weights is dangerous, try being weak. Being weak is dangerous. —BRET CONTRERAS

One overriding reason to seek professional guidance, at least in the beginning phase of weight training, is simple: to avoid injury.

Strength training is not inherently dangerous, but a mistake of ignorance can result in serious injury. There are a hundred ways to perform each exercise—and almost as many ways to hurt yourself. Particularly with free weights, it is essential that you learn the safest technique for each exercise.

The most common injury in upper body routines is to the shoulder. A good way to protect yourself from this all too common injury is to practice a "locked shoulder" position for all weight-bearing exercises involving your upper body. This means stabilizing the shoulders by keeping them down and back during exercises like pulls ups or bench presses, not allowing them to stretch to the end of their range of motion. Keeping your elbows in instead of splayed out reduces strain on shoulder components. Unlike your elbows and knees, the shoulders don't have a natural "locked" position. Bearing weight to the end of your shoulder's range of motion is a set up for a debilitating rotator cuff injury. With *all* resistance training, stop any exercise that causes pain or clicking.

Another general rule: avoid holding your breath while lifting weights. Steady, deep nasal breathing during the weight movement not only prevents dizziness, it induces the state of mindfulness that will help you focus on the exercise. Use your breathing rate to time your positive/negative (ascending/descending) movements. Focus on slow, steady repetitions.

As you'll see, training with less weight is not only more efficient, it reduces your exposure to injury. Instead of straining to move the absolute maximum weight you can handle, find a lesser weight which you can *slo-o-o-wly* move through enough repetitions—something over seven and less than twelve—to the failure point.

MASTERY

Slo-o-o-o-w is Faster, Less is More

Slow. You'll hear this repeated like a mantra in Mastery. Whether it's running, swimming, stretching, lifting weights—the best results come from slow, protracted, steady tension.

In strength training, slower repetitions—a minimum of ten seconds through the positive/negative cycle of each exercise—without stopping between reps means you use less weight for a longer period. Lesser weight, fewer reps, performed *slooooowly*. No quick, jerky snatches, no use of momentum. No bouncing off a stopping point at the end of each movement. Your objective is *not* to hoist the maximum amount of weight. Using less weight puts less stress on the joints and reduces the chance of injury or strain.

The actual weight and the device—dumbbell, machine, pull up bar—are ancillary details. They are simply tools to provide resistance to challenge your target muscle. In every resistance exercise, let your focus begin and end not on the weight but on the target muscle. Staying focused means you keep the target muscle flexed, under tension, throughout the set of repetitions.

To stay focused, avoid distractions. One of the downsides of health clubs is the temptation to socialize with other members or to lock on to a mindless television program while you're working out. The better you're able to direct your concentration on the objective—the flexing of the target muscle—the more impressive will be the results.

But wait a minute, you say. *What exactly is a target muscle?*

Good question. Resistance training, unlike most other sports activities, concentrates on one muscle at a time. No teaming up with muscle groups. To produce the best results, try to invoke a monk-like concentration on the muscle you're exercising. All else—the weight, the bench, even your hands—play support roles. They are tools to assist you in the objective of flexing the target muscle.

Begin the power stroke by flexing the target muscle—*and keeping it flexed*—until failure. Concentrate on powering up from this muscle rather than from the hand holding the weight or bar. It's this ongoing tension, focusing on the isolated muscle, that produces results. Relaxing the flex between reps, as most people do, reduces the effectiveness of the exercise and makes you more vulnerable to injury. In this seemingly paradoxical way, you build strength and grow muscle by tearing down muscle tissue so that it can rebuild itself in stronger and firmer shape.

Okay, but how much weight do I use?

Less than you may think. With almost every fitness protocol, resistance or aerobic training, less is more, particularly at the outset of your training. Lesser weight, fewer reps, performed *slooooowly* are the key to success. Perform each repetition, no matter whether it's a biceps curl, bench press, pull down, at a cadence of five seconds in each direction without pausing between reps. The idea is to maintain the tension on the target muscle until failure—the point at which you can no longer suspend the weight. If you've begun with the correct weight, this should occur after the seventh repetition and should keep the target muscle under tension for 90 to 120 seconds.

How many sets (one set=six to twelve reps) should you do? If you perform the exercises as prescribed, working the target muscle to failure, then one set of each is your objective. After trial and error, you may find it useful to do warm up reps before performing the actual rep-to-fail exercise. If so, use a lighter weight, no more than 60% of the exercise weight. Allow no more than a minute of rest while you add the target weight, and then exercise to your fail point.

If you've done it correctly—taken your reps to the failure point—you're finished with that exercise. Move on to another muscle group, but do not re-engage the muscles you've already exercised. That minute-and-a-half of high tension, working each targeted muscle to failure, is the key to the desired result—breaking down the muscle tissue so that it can rebuild itself in a stronger version. Resist the temptation to return to that exercise and repeat.

When you can perform more than your original number reps-to-fail, then add weight, but in small increments. No more than ten pounds or ten percent of the original.

You'll work other groups of muscles similarly—biceps, pectorals, shoulders, then perhaps the quads (the big muscles atop your thighs)—reaching the fail point for each groups. Then let these muscles rest and rebuild at least three days while you target other muscles. Make sure to give yourself at least two days a week with no weight work while your body restores itself. A good routine, especially for beginners, is to do resistance training three days a week, using the days in between for aerobic activity, and take one full day off with no demanding exercise.

For sure, there will be days on which you can't make the target number of reps. Don't be concerned. This is a signal that you've overshot your current target or, more likely, that your muscles haven't fully recovered from the previous workout. Don't push it. Your body is talking to you. Lower the weight, call it a day, and allow the overstressed muscle to fully rebuild.

Is the reps-to-fail technique right for everyone? Certainly not. This routine—slow reps and lesser weight, working to a fail point—has a different objective and produces a different result than the classic body builders' protocol. No, you won't attain Incredible Hulk proportions from this routine. Nor should it be a substitute for sport-specific workouts. The reps-to-fail protocol is aimed at the senior athlete whose mission is to grow strength and muscle mass.

Failure *IS* an Option

Failure? In a Mastery mission?

Yes, absolutely. In fact, the objective of the slow rep/low weight training technique *is* to fail. And "failure" in slow cadence resistance training can be the most difficult aspect for beginners to embrace, at least mentally. It doesn't mean you quit at the point where your muscle has become fatigued. It means, to quote *The 4-Hour Body* author Tim Ferris, "pushing like you have a gun to your head." Pushing until you can't push anymore. And then pushing some more. Pushing until the muscle trembles. Then trying to sustain the tension for another five seconds.

Hard work? Without doubt. Unpleasant? Only in the beginning. Only until you've made the mental adaptation to the technique. How do you know if you've reached the failure point? If you've rested a few minutes after the set and then feel as if you can do another, then you didn't work hard enough the first time around. It's that last rep—the one you sustained while you gasped and your muscle quivered—that delivers the payoff. All the previous reps were preliminary. By attaining this level of muscle tension, literally breaking down the tissue so that it can rebuild, you grow new muscle mass. And new strength.

Does this push you out of your comfort zone? Perhaps, but after you've become familiar with the failure point it will no longer intimidate you. You may be pleasantly surprised at the Zen-like state you enter, feeling a sense of detachment, breaking through what you thought was a physical limitation. You will find it enlightening—and liberating. Your workouts will become purposeful and, believe it or not, more rewarding. Best of all, the results will be apparent.

Where to Train

Take care of your body. It's the only place you have to live.
–JIM ROHN

What is the ideal venue for weight training? Fitness center? Home gym? Should you hire a private trainer?

MASTERY

Let your schedule, life style, and social proclivities determine which is best. Good health clubs and fitness centers have top notch equipment. Most have resident trainers who can offer professional advice. The downside, beyond paying a membership fee, is that you have to suit up and make a special trip to the facility. At peak hours you may be waiting in line for the machine you want to use. In most health clubs you'll be surrounded by other members, many of whom regard fitness training as a social activity. Blaring televisions, piped-in music, and the commotion of group training go with the territory. For many, the fitness motivation vanishes when the newness of the club membership wears off. The inconvenience and nuisance value aren't worth it.

If the health club scene doesn't appeal to you, consider a home fitness facility. A basic set of equipment doesn't have to occupy a large space and will quickly pay for itself over the cost of a health club. To train with free weights you'll need a weight bench (or any bench of similar dimensions) and a set of dumbbells. Basic dumbbells are the lowest-tech equipment in the game. The cheapest option is the hex-ended, cast iron or vinyl-covered version that comes in all weights and are obtainable from discount stores like Wal-Mart and Target and sports store such as Dick's and Sports Authority. Depending on your size and strength, dumbbells of fifteen, twenty, and perhaps thirty pounds should be sufficient. A slightly more expensive and space-saving option is an adjustable set such as the compact versions sold by PowerBlock or Bowflex.

Or . . . if space and expense are no object, you can invest in a high-tech, multi-station home gym unit. These units come in all varieties and degrees of sophistication. All in one machines such as the Body-Solid devices, Weider Pro, or Bowflex range in price from a few hundred dollars to several thousand and are an alternative to a bench and rack and a room full of free weights.

There's yet another option: the classic and equipment-free method of using your own body weight. Old-fashioned pull ups exercise the back, chest, shoulders, arms, and abs. For a chinning bar, you can install one of the door or wall-mounted models marketed by Everlast or ProSource. The bars can be screwed with brackets into a wall stud or suspended by leverage over a doorway.

Even more classic is the traditional boot camp style push up. Performed in the slow rep-to-fail protocol, push ups are as potent as any weight device for developing shoulders, upper arms, even abdominal muscles. The beauty of the humble push up is that it requires zero equipment and can be done anywhere—home, hotel room, the office.

The Llama walk

Few bodyweight workouts deliver as great a payoff as leg exercise. Because the largest muscles in your body are in your legs, strengthening those muscles fires up your overall metabolism. One of the simplest and best ways to strengthen the upper leg muscles is an ancient exercise—a variation of the modern lunge—called the Llama Walk.

Here's how to do it:

— *Step forward with your left foot as if you were taking a strong forward stride. Swing your right hand forward simultaneously. Dip as you step, lowering your right knee to just behind your left heel. Your left leg should be bent at a 90° angle, your knee directly over your foot.*

— *Rise to the vertical and step forward with your right foot as you raise your left hand. Repeat on opposite sides as many times as is comfortable.*

To avoid soreness, start with just a few repetitions until your quads have adapted. When you're ready you can up the ante by carrying a dumbbell in each hand while you do the walk. Again, start with the minimum weight, then work up.

Exercising these large muscles stimulates the release of growth hormones that can increase overall muscle mass. Strengthening the large leg muscles also helps head off knee problems, improves balance, and will translate into greater endurance for your other fitness missions.

<>

Almost as elegant in their simplicity are resistance bands, or resistance tubes as they are called in some versions. They are essentially large rubber bands with a handle on either end. The bands come in a range of resistance levels from easily stretchable to iron-solid. With the bands you exercise muscle groups in much the same way as using dumbbells or bar bells. For instance, one handle can be held down with the foot while you grip the other handle and perform biceps curls. Or loop the band around a column or sturdy support at chest height and, with your back to the bands, grip the handles and push forward as in a standing chest press. With a bit of imagination, you can replicate almost every weight station work out with the bands. The beauty of resistance bands is that they can be stuffed into your suitcase or shoulder bag and used almost anywhere you travel.

One subtle difference between bands and weights: both are resistance trainers, but the resistance with weights is provided by gravity, whereas the resistance in the bands comes from their elasticity. While the resistance from gravity remains mostly constant throughout the movement, the resistance from bands reaches its maximum at the far extreme of the movement. With a little practice and experimentation you'll find the ideal band resistance for a slow rep-to-failure work out.

In case you haven't noticed yet, there's a hidden truth sandwiched into the many options of fitness training equipment. Money isn't king. Nor is hardware. The difference in results between spending megabucks and small change is minimal. Your best results from fitness training come not from exotic equipment or expensive memberships but from your commitment.

Measuring Results

What gets measured gets managed.
—Peter Drucker

Whether you're considering running, strength training, swimming, or a combination of protocols, approach the fitness mission the same way you approach any mission. Analyze the activity. Assess your capabilities. Determine the suitability of the mission.

Does it make sense for you? Is it realistic? Is the mission a go?

If so, be sure to set achievable goals. Assign a time frame. To achieve the desired results, your schedule must be reasonable and doable. And those results must be measurable.

How do you measure results? You guessed it. Record keeping. From day one in your fitness mission, log your progress. Record in your journal or in a separate log the data from each session—distance, times, laps, weights, reps. Use the same log to record body statistics. Are you adding muscle mass? Gaining or losing weight? Reducing body fat percentage?

As with all your journals, you are writing for *you*. Your fitness log is where you insert observations about the mission—which exercises are best, which are most difficult, what works and what doesn't as well as your innermost thoughts.

Why am I doing this? How does this exercise make me feel? Am I achieving the results I expected? If not, why not?

When the inevitable fatigue sets in and you confront obstacles on your course to fitness, your log will help keep you focused. The pages of accumulated results will serve to remind you why you chose this mission. They'll help keep you on the road to Mastery.

---

1   "In four weeks, you'll get stronger—you can feel yourself take out the trash or carry groceries with more ease," reported Dr. Miriam Nelson, director of the Center for Physical Activity and Attrition at Tufts in an article posted on the *21 Minute Fit for Life* site. "In four to six weeks, you might see less pain with arthritis."

2   "Only men who did weights had the younger muscle mass," concluded sarcopenia researcher Dr. William Evans at the University of Arkansas for Medical Sciences, referring to the Denmark study comparing men in their sixties—weight trainers vs. swimmers and runners.

3   According to the National Osteoporosis Foundation, Caucasian women between the ages of twenty and eighty lose one-third of their bone density in their hip. African-American women have less density loss, but at least thirty-five percent are estimated to have low bone mass, meaning their bones are getting weaker. Women who are lactose intolerant are especially vulnerable because they may be getting insufficient calcium.

4   Felicia Cosman, MD, a spokeswoman for the National Osteoporosis Foundation says, "If you persist with your weight training, even a one percent change in bone density every year adds up to a ten percent difference after ten years . . . That's a lot of bone."

Part Three

Peak Health

When health is absent, wisdom cannot reveal itself, art cannot manifest, strength cannot fight, wealth becomes useless, and intelligence cannot be applied.
— HEROPHILUS

He who has health has hope; and he who has hope has everything.
—ARABIC PROVERB

ROBERT GANDT AND GARY A. SCOTT

11

The Nutrition Mission

The doctor of the future will no longer treat the human frame with drugs, but rather will cure and prevent disease with nutrition.
—THOMAS EDISON

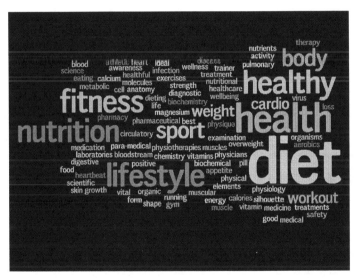

Shutterstock 281626106

Vitality, mental agility, physical fitness — all are critical components in fulfilling your missions. But each of these components, to be effective, requires fuel. The *right* fuel, meaning *nutrition*. Or, more simply, meaning what you eat—and what you *don't* eat.

As in . . . *diet.*

At this point you may be rolling your eyeballs. *Diet?* For most of your adult life you've been hearing about the latest fad diet—low-carb diet, high-protein diet, paleo diet, gluten-free diet, low-fat diet, vegan diet. Each comes with anecdotal proof that it is the *best* way to lose weight, gain muscle mass, feel more energetic, live longer, have better sex.

And what's remarkable is that *each* claim may have some truth to it.

Hence the question: How can these different diets, some with dramatically contradictory regimens, all work?

The Answer: Each works *some* of the time. And sometimes they don't work at all. Sometimes they even produce the opposite effect the dieter wants.

The truth is, there is no single "best" diet. You are a unique human being with unique dietary requirements. Instead of an official best diet, what you need is knowledge. You need to know precisely how nutrition can help the unique human being that is *you* in the accomplishment of your missions. Your ideal diet should be molded around an array of factors: your body type, your current physical imbalances, your environmental surroundings, the types of available fresh food, your schedule, routine and lifestyle. And, most certainly, the particular requirements of your mission.

That's right, we're back to *mission*. As with all other aspects of Mastery, it helps to frame these highly generalized subjects—health, fitness, nutrition—in the context of *mission*. Instead of assigning yourself a vague objective such as *I want to be fit*, or *I want to be healthy*, be specific. What do you want to achieve in terms of nutrition, health, lifestyle? Put a definition, a number, a measurable quantity to it.

For example:

I want . . . to weigh 165 pounds.
I want . . . an LDL-Cholesterol number of less than 100 mg/dl.
I want . . . a thirty-two-inch waist.
I want . . . a blood pressure reading of 120/70.

I want . . . the energy to run three miles without feeling fatigued.

I want . . . a maximum blood sugar level of 80.

I want . . . (fill in the blank and be specific).

Be realistic. Fit your goal to what you know is achievable. Then do your homework. If your mission, for example, is to lose weight—a supremely worthwhile mission—you'll probably limit your calories to 1,200 to 1,800 a day. If your mission is to compete in an ironman triathlon, your burn count might soar to 7,000 to 10,000.

You are in control. Make nutrition match your mission.

Here's another basic truism: Your physical well-being and your mental well-being are interrelated. The mind-body is a two-component, interconnected unit. Whether your mission is physical or mental, nutrition—meaning eating right—is an essential component in reaching your goal.

What does this mean to the pursuer of Mastery? That good health is critical in the accomplishment of your missions. And good health starts with *nutrition*.

Nutrition is the missing link. Despite the fad diets and miracle pills and magazine covers featuring slinky bodies, nutrition remains at the bottom of Americans' collective consciousness. They are deluged with temptations for fast foods—burgers, fries, colas, doughnuts—and worse.

A Business Week article, "Why More Extreme Foods Are Creeping Onto Menus" reports:

Now a doughnut sandwich is available for a lucky (or brave) few at none other than Dunkin' Donuts. The chain is testing a Glazed Donut Breakfast Sandwich—there's a pepper fried egg and cherrywood-smoked bacon inside—in about a dozen stores in the Boston area.

The Glazed Donut Breakfast Sandwich is one of many curious new items offered by restaurant chains, often for a limited time, to attract that adventure-seeking, fast-food-eating creature known as the young American male. And who do you think is chugging Johnny Rockets' Big Apple Shake? (That's the one with an entire slice of apple pie blended into a milkshake with 1,140 calories and 37 grams of saturated fat.)

Should anyone be shocked that the United States tops the list of most obese citizens in the world? Any doubt why Americans' longevity rates lag behind most developed countries?

But *you're* not obese, right? You don't exist on a diet of Egg McMuffins sprinkled with sugar. You have an idea of what constitutes a healthy diet, and you try to limit your calorie intake to . . . well, something not outrageous.

But life is busy. You travel, you work, you eat on the run. Of all the things that occupy your attention, what you eat is far from the top of the list.

Here are more truisms: Obesity—with its related consequences—is a choice. An unhealthy lifestyle is a choice. A shortened life span due to improper nutrition is a choice. And a healthy, vibrant lifestyle is—that's right—a choice.

One of the prime objectives of Mastery is to live a life by design. *Your* design. There are few areas of your life over which you have more control than nutrition, and there are few aspects of your existence that respond so dramatically to change. All you need to apply these changes to your lifestyle are knowledge and the will to implement them.

First comes the knowledge.

Balance, Combine, Chew

You already know the effects of junk food and fast burning carbohydrates: obesity, toxicity, hormonal disturbances caused by an excess of insulin. You also know, at least in principle, that a diet of healthy food, correctly eaten, produces the opposite effect: improved digestion, reduced weight, increased energy, reduced toxicity and a balance of the hormonal system. Cravings and excessive hunger disappear. You possess high energy.

Okay, improving the quality of your diet is important, but it's only part of the quotient. Even if you eat the right amount of the best food in the world, you still miss most of the critical nutrients if your digestive system isn't working correctly. Nutrition is a combination of *what* you eat and *how* you digest it.

Here are the seven basic ways to make eating more nutritional.

— *Eat a balance of fat, carbohydrates and protein.*

— *Eat combinations of food for ideal digestion.*

— *Eat at the right times.*

— *Eat the right amount.*

— *Chew in the right way.*

— *Replace sugar and flour with quinoa and stevia.*

— *balance out pH.*

Balancing Act

A balance of fat, carbohydrates and protein—this is the ideal way to maintain protein balance. And how do you achieve this balance without consuming excessive amounts of meat?

Here's a good way: replace the meat intake with quinoa, eggs, cheese, yoghurt.

Much of Americans' epidemic of poor health and stress can be blamed on hormonal disturbances caused by an excess production of insulin. And like most diet-related disorders, it's a result of excessive food intake and/or a lopsided protein-carbohydrate-fat balance.

Every time you consume food, hormones in your body change. An overload of carbs or protein produces hormonal changes for the worse. A quality diet with a balance of three parts carbohydrate, two parts protein, one part fat has the power to produce beneficial effects.

In his ground-breaking book *Enter the Zone*,[1] Dr. Barry Sears, former Massachusetts Institute of Technology researcher, blew away most of the myths about carbs, protein, sugar, cholesterol, fat. Sears's approach shunned the fast-burning carbohydrates that produce blood sugar spikes and excessive insulin. The Zone diet balanced the intake of protein, good (low-glycemic) carbohydrates, and a moderate amount of monounsaturated fats and drew on stored body fat to produce energy.

While Sears's protein-over-carbs platform was nothing new, his approach made it palatable to readers who had grown wary of quack nutritionists and diets-du-jour that worked for a while but turned out to be unsustainable.

With lists of good and bad carbohydrates and easy-to-follow food blocks and recipes, the Zone regimen had the potential to roll back obesity, heart disease, diabetes, and many forms of cancer.

Did it work? Beautifully — but only for those who actually stuck to the diet. Most Americans didn't. In the years since balanced carb/protein diets have been in vogue, the U. S.'s title of "World's Fattest People" has only became more secure.

Will it work for you? Let's see.

Good Combos, Bad Combos

For purposes of combining, foods fall into three categories: neutral, savory, and sweet. Here's how they can be mixed—or not mixed:

— **Neutral**

Foods in the neutral category can be mixed with savory or sweet, but savory and sweet foods should *not* be mixed. The principal neutral foods are grains, cereals, nuts and seeds. Cereals and nuts can be ground, soaked with water, then drained to improve their digestibility.

— **Savory**

This category includes meat and most vegetables. Savory spices include salt, pepper, chilies, oregano, coriander, bay leaf, cumin, saffron, and fennel.

— **Sweet**

Fruits are sweet. Sweet spices include cinnamon, nutmeg, allspice, ginger, mint.

According to ancient nutritionists, no two fats should be mixed, nor two fruit types. For example, oranges and grapefruit, being the same type, can be eaten together, as can apples and pears, blackberries and strawberries. Different types like oranges and apples should be avoided, as should melon and pineapple.

The noble banana is in a category by itself. Bananas should be eaten alone or only with dairy. (Bananas, by the way, should *not* be cooked).

Nutritional experts tell us that another combination to avoid is salt and sugar, which are hard to digest when consumed together. Meals should be one or the other, sweet or salty, using spices like ginger to stimulate the digestive system.

Timing is Everything

Though *what* you eat is important, almost as critical is *when* you eat. The timing of your meals should be tuned to your activity, to the phase of the day, even to the seasons.

Morning and evening meals, according to nutritionists, should be sweet. The noon meal, which ought to be the largest of the day, is usually salt.

Numerous ancient dietary disciplines break the day into the three cycles: fire, earth, and air.

— *2AM TO 6AM: The Air Cycle.* Wake up time. The mind is light and active—the perfect time to think, multi task, and learn.

— *6AM TO 10AM: The Water Cycle.* Strength is increased. The perfect time to do physical activity (for a better workout with less chance of injury)

— *10AM TO 2PM: The Fire Cycle.* Time for digestion. High noon is the optimum time for the main meal of the day.

— *2PM TO 6PM: The next Air Cycle.* Your mind is light and active again. The best time for study and mental work.

— *6PM TO 10PM: The next Water Cycle.* The best way to fall into the first deep REM sleep cycle is to be asleep before 10PM.

— *10PM TO 2AM: The next Fire Cycle.* The best time for deep sleep. If you eat a heavy evening meal, this cycle will digest it. However if an evening meal is early and light, this second fire cycle acts like an oven cleaner. Stresses and toxicities gained during the day are burned up, adding energy for the morning and insuring a body that is not overweight

To Everything a Season

Live in each season as it passes: breathe the air, drink the drink, taste the fruit.
— HENRY DAVID THOREAU

One of the reasons the various diets—high carb, high protein, low calorie, Paleo—all come with unimpeachable evidence that they work is because *they do work*—but only *part of the time*, each for about four months a year. In his book *The 3- Season Diet,*[2] John Douillard argues that by eating foods appropriate to the season, you obtain the best of the several conflicting diets.

In pre-industrial times, before refrigeration and high speed transport, nature provided a seasonally adjusted diet. The main supply of food in the spring was exactly what the human body required. Radishes are an example. A revered food in many ancient nutritional disciplines, light and spicy radishes were usually the first crop available in spring and also happened to be a natural stimulant for digestion.

Derived from a 5,000-year-old traditional medical system, the 3-season diet refers to the three growing seasons of the year—spring, summer, and fall. The diet for each season ranges from low calorie—low fat in the spring, high carbohydrate in summer, high protein in winter.

The varying diets conform to your body's natural response to the changing seasons. For example, in the summer when the days are long and hot, you require cooling, high-energy foods such as fruits, berries, melons, vegetables—a naturally high carbohydrate diet.

By late autumn and winter your body's cravings turn to fats and heavier foods such as soups, nuts, warm grains, pumpkins, squash, and high fat and protein foods such as meat and fish.

Spring is the sluggish season for your digestion, and that's when you need a good clean out. This is the time of year when your body favors salads, berries, and leafy greens—a naturally low-fat diet.

Making seasonal adaptations is a natural way to lose weight, beat the food cravings that defeat most diets, and get fit.

But there's more to timing than the calendar. Not only should your diet be tuned to the season, but also the time of day. Keeping calories down and eating only on an empty stomach are keys to healthy digestion. Begin the day with an easily digestible breakfast, then try to leave at least four hours between meals

Scientific evidence suggests the value of eating in pleasant surroundings. Good moods and good food make for good digestion. Nobel Prize-winning neuroscientist Candace Pert, Ph.D, postulated that the entity we call the mind resides not just in the brain but in the entire body. By Pert's reasoning, the mind and the body communicate using the chemistry of emotion. Short chains of amino acids called peptides and receptors, located in the brain, stomach, muscles, glands and all major organs, provide the message link between mind and body.

You know the feeling. When you're happy, your entire body is happy. As you've proven to yourself a thousand times, your digestion—good or bad—is directly affected by the chemistry of the mood and moment.

For this reason, what you do immediately *after* you eat affects how your food is digested. Light physical activity following a meal aids digestion, burns up blood sugar, and heads off those 10:30 A.M and 3:30 P.M. crashes that leave you craving carbohydrates.

In one scientific study, researchers looked for physiological differences between subjects' exercising before and after meals. Their test subjects performed only low intensity exercises—walking 1.2 miles in about half an hour, then doing fifteen repetitions with light (five to six- pound) dumbbells in eight positions.

Results? The pre-meal exercise reduced the subjects' triglyceride levels by 25%. The post-meal exercise produced a more dramatic result—*a drop of 72%.*

In another study conducted by the Mayo Clinic, two groups of subjects, one with type 1 diabetes, and the other group without, were taken on walks after two of their daily meals. Following the third meal, which was picked at random, they remained stationary. In every instance the subjects—both diabetics and non-diabetics— showed lower blood glucose levels when they walked than when they didn't.

The study's overwhelming conclusion: light exercise after any meal, even a task as minimal as washing dishes, had the effect of *lowering* blood glucose levels.

The Fine Art of Chewing

All life is an experiment. The more experiments you make the better.
—RALPH WALDO EMERSON

Here's an experiment that seems almost too simple to be effective. *Chewing.* But chewing in a different way.

First, the underlying science.

Correct chewing (we'll describe that soon) releases nutrient molecules, allowing energy from food to be quickly released, prompting your brain to recognize flavors and release the appropriate digestive fluids. If done properly, chewing stimulates the sphincters.

Sphincters? Aren't we talking about chewing? Umm, yes, but the sphincters are *all* the ring-shaped muscles that surround the various orifices of your body. They include muscles around the eyes, the nostrils, the mouth, the anus, the urethra and the genitals. In a healthy body the ring muscles work together, contracting and relaxing simultaneously. They activate the respiratory system, the gastrointestinal system, the circulatory system, the lymphatic system, the musculoskeletal system, and the urogenital system. The ring muscles are ultimately responsible for putting all the other muscles and organs of the body to work.

In *Secret of the Ring Muscles* [3] author Paula Garbourg contended that sphincter exercises can reduce or eliminate a host of problems ranging from asthma to back aches to depression. But the single ring muscle exercise that has the most power to affect your digestion and weight control is—that's right—*chewing*.

Here's how to do it, according to Garbourg:

Chewing should be done with the lips closed, but with the oral cavity open as wide as possible. When chewing is done correctly the lower sphincters and intestines can be felt working in rhythm and causing the abdomen to contract.

With proper exercise the sphincters return to normal operation and there is no longer a demand for more food than the body needs. It is possible to eat enough without the fear of getting fat. All you have to do is to make sure to open your jaws widely enough with each chew to bring all the sphincter muscles into action. This will reduce your body's craving to eat and will also enable your body to burn up more calories more efficiently.

Garbourg believed that when the sphincter muscles are out of balance, your body tries to restore them via the act of chewing.

Thus what seems to be a craving for food may actually be a craving for proper exercise of the ring muscles.

Can something as simple as changing how you chew be a weight control technique? A means to better health? Yes, according to many who have tried it.

Will it work for you? Very possibly. Again, you are unique. Remember that the essence of Mastery is exploring paths that may lead you to a higher state of health, ability, knowledge. Of the many experiments you conduct during that journey, this may be the least complicated. And the most risk-free. No investment, no club to join, no life style change. All you have to do is chew.

Meet the Carb Busters

It's an ongoing war: you versus your cravings. And one of your toughest, most entrenched cravings is the one you have for fast burning carbohydrates. You know the usual suspects: sweet foods and drinks, white bread and other processed high glycemic carbohydrates. They're the ones that cause the abrupt spikes and drops in blood sugar. At the same time they activate the parts of your brain linked to hunger, craving, and reward.

When these foods raise your blood sugar level, your body reacts by producing insulin, which in turn causes the blood sugar to plummet. That highly caloric, quickly absorbed food you just consumed has stimulated the main reward and pleasure center of the brain, and now you *crave* food that will restore the level quickly. And while this is a normal cycle, it becomes a cycle of overeating driven by those high-glycemic foods.

There are two major villains in this blood sugar/insulin saga: sugar and flour. Fortunately for you, replacements are on the way. They're called quinoa and stevia.

Quinoa

Pronounced *keen-wa*, it was considered the mother of all grains by the Incas living in the high Andes. Quinoa is one of the few crops that thrive in the thin air and extreme temperatures. This super food is a high protein grain replacement and one of the few vegetable sources to offer a complete protein. Quinoa also contains a fair amount of Omega-3 essential fatty acids.

Quinoa makes a good replacement for flour, rice and corn, the holy trinity in food producers' glucose armory. Quinoa is also a suitable stand-in for cereals and pasta.

The World Health Organization gives quinoa a protein rating on the order of milk. The United Nations has classified quinoa as a super crop based on its nutritional value and high protein content.

While quinoa is usually considered to be a whole grain, it is actually a seed. A relative of spinach, beets and chard, quinoa is a great vegetarian food. And because it is gluten free, quinoa is an ideal substitute for anyone suffering from wheat and grass family allergies.

Quinoa is also a source of phosphorus, magnesium, zinc, copper and manganese, Vitamins B6, Niacin, Thiamin, and has high levels of lysine - an essential amino acid for creating protein. Plus it is low in fat and an excellent source of complex carbohydrates.

Could Quinoa be the miracle food?

Not for everyone. For the vast majority of people, quinoa is a safe and nutritious food, but it does contain three substances that could cause unwanted reactions in some people. One is saponins, soap-like molecules that coat the exterior of quinoa, and can lead to digestive problems. Another is prolamins, a protein group found in some grains, including wheat, which can cause gluten reactions even though quinoa is technically gluten free. A third substance is phytic acid, which has the potential to bind to important minerals such as zinc and magnesium and make them unavailable to your body.

A good way to remove most of the unwanted substances is to prepare the quinoa just as the Incas did. Soak and ferment the grain before you cook it. Soaking quinoa for twelve hours removes most of the saponins as well as 60% to 70% of the phytic acid. Fermenting the quinoa with whey for eighteen hours removes even more of the phytic acid.

Stevia to the Rescue

The average American consumes about five hundred extra calories a day from sugar.[4] Most of the sugar comes from soft drinks, fast food, and desserts. Besides weight gain from the empty calories, high sugar intake is linked to an increased incidence of heart disease. A 2013 report in the *Journal of the American Heart Association* offered compelling evidence that sugar had a damaging effect on the pumping mechanism of your heart and could increase the chances of heart failure.

But heart disease is not the only downside of sugar. High sugar intake triggers brisk insulin secretion, which in turn leads to increased demand on insulin production and insulin resistance in the body's cells. Excessive sugar intake is associated with an increased risk of cancer, diabetes, impaired immune system, acne, even myopia. Perhaps scariest of all is a 2012 study linking excess sugar consumption to deficiencies in memory and declines in overall cognitive health.

Okay, you say, the case against sugar is convincing. But how do you overcome an addiction to sweetness that seems to be hardwired in your genes? Is there a suitable alternative?

Several. But most low-cal sweeteners are artificial, and some come with their own dangerous side effects. Of the few natural sweeteners, one of them—stevia—has become immensely popular. For good reason. Stevia *tastes* sweet, on a par with other sugar substitutes. It comes from the leaves of the plant species *stevia rebaudiana* and is native to South America where it has been used for medicinal purposes for centuries.

Though Stevia is up to 300 times sweeter than sugar, it has a zero glycemic index (meaning no carbs), no artificial ingredients, and produces a negligible effect on your blood sugar.

Stevia comes in liquid and powder form. You can add it to your smoothie, coffee, tea. You can use it as a sugar substitute for baking. A single teaspoon of stevia extract, depending on the brand, can have the same sweetening effect as a *whole cup* of sugar.

The stevia plant is easy to grow yourself. It thrives in most moderate climates, and a small planting produces enough leaves for a large supply of stevia for your own use. Check out sites like *Mother Earth News* [5] for how to grow and harvest stevia plants.

The pH Factor

Most natural health and nutrition experts agree that a balanced body pH is vital to your health. Here's a refresher on the pH factor and how it affects your health.

The pH, which stands for potential hydrogen, is a measurement of relative alkalinity to acidity. The range is 0-14, and your blood pH should be within the narrow band of 7.35—7.4. If the blood pH moves below 6.8 or above 7.8, the result can be convulsions, coma, and death. Your body responds powerfully to pH changes by drawing calcium from other parts of the body (such as bones) to buffer the blood pH. When the blood's pH balance is compromised, resulting in a condition called "acidosis," diseases ranging from cardiovascular problems to high LDL cholesterol to osteoporosis may result.

According to most nutritionists, the single largest influencer of your body's pH is diet. Everything you eat is either alkaline or acidic. Thumbnail rule: high-glycemic foods increase acidity, low-glycemic drops it. Meat, coffee, sodas, most processed food, and alcohol all tilt the balance toward acidic. Diets high in vegetables, legumes, raw greens, and whole grains tend to keep the balance more alkaline.

Other factors such as stress, lack of exercise, and insufficient sleep also tilt the acid-alkaline balance. A sedentary lifestyle tends to worsen acidosis, which takes you on a downward spiral, decreasing energy and making exercise even more difficult.

Here is a brief list of the most common alkaline-producing foods and liquids:

— **Alkalizing Vegetables**

Alfalfa, barley grass, beet greens, beets, broccoli, cabbage, carrot, cauliflower, celery, chard greens, chlorella, collard greens, cucumber, dandelions, eggplant, fermented veggies, garlic, green beans, green peas, kale, kohlrabi, lettuce, mushrooms, mustard greens, nightshade veggies, onions, parsnips, peas, peppers, pumpkin, radishes, rutabaga, sea veggies, spinach greens, spirulina, sprouts, sweet potatoes, tomatoes, watercress, wheat grass, wild greens.

— **Alkalizing Fruits:**

Apple, apricot, avocado, banana, berries, blackberries, cantaloupe, cherries, coconut, currants, dates, dried figs, grapes, grapefruit, honeydew melon, lemon, lime, mango, muskmelons, nectarine, orange, peach, pear, pineapple, raisins raspberries, rhubarb, strawberries, tangerine, tomato, tropical fruits, umeboshi plums, watermelon, almonds, chestnuts, millet, tempeh (fermented), tofu (fermented),

— **Alkalizing Sweeteners & Spices**

Stevia (but *not* most other artificial sweeteners), chili pepper, cinnamon, curry, ginger, herbs (all), miso, mustard, sea salt, tamari.

— Water Ionizers

Another way to add alkalinity into the body, though expensive and without strong clinical evidence, is with ionized alkaline water created by water ionizers. These water ionizing devices treat water with electrical current and purport to make the pH around 8 to 9. Do water ionizers work? Perhaps. The science is still thin, but the devices have gained a large number of faithful users.

— Other Alkalizers

Here are some others: Alkaline antioxidant water, apple cider vinegar, bee pollen, fresh fruit juice, green juices, lecithin granules, mineral water, blackstrap molasses, probiotic cultures, soured dairy products, veggie juices.

Citrus fruits contain citric acid that has an alkalinizing effect in the system because a food's pH activity in the body is not related to the pH of the food itself. Lemons are actually acidic, but are alkaline-forming in the body. Meat, on the other hand, is alkaline before digestion, but is highly acid forming in the body.

Numerous alkalizing supplements are available, mostly in health food stores. One of these is green food powder, made from various types of grasses, wheat, and barley. Diluted with water the powder makes good-tasting smoothies and can help alkalize your body. Calcium supplements, which come in all sizes and forms, are a natural anti-acid mineral which help restore calcium lost from your body. Also available are various formulations of pH alkalizing liquid or powder, most of which contain alkaline mineral salts such as potassium, magnesium, calcium, and iron. One of these, a popular supplement called <u>Alkaline Plus</u>, promises that its proprietary formula causes the body to naturally produce additional amounts of alkaline.

While none of these supplements is a substitute for a healthy diet and lifestyle, they can assist in making your body chemistry more alkaline.

Does pH-specific eating and drinking really work? As in almost every area of nutrition, there are dissenting opinions. Though the science is inconclusive as to *how much* or even *whether* the body's pH can be shifted purely by diet, what seems clear is that a diet low in acid-producing foods—meat and cheese—and high in alkalizing foods—veggies and fruit—*does* help prevent many major health calamities associated with acidosis: kidney stones, colon cancer, type 2 diabetes, and contributes to healthy heart and brain function.

What should *you* do? The same as in every aspect of Mastery: Do your own homework. If you find the evidence compelling, consider putting fresh vegetables and fruits at the center of your diet. From that step, you may then choose to eat whatever amounts of nutrient-dense foods that *you* know from your ongoing experiments work best for you.

Alkaline Potassium Broth

Here's a good-tasting concoction that will improve your body's alkalinity. Potassium broth can help flush your body of unwanted toxins while adding vitamins and minerals to your diet. The broth makes a particularly good addition during a fast (which we talk about later) or a detox. This basic recipe can be supplemented with other mineral-rich ingredients:

— 4 organic, well scrubbed potatoes
— 3 organic carrots, peeled and chopped
— 4 organic celery stalks, chopped
— 1 bunch organic parsley

— 4 quarts filtered water

Prepare by chopping the vegetables and placing them in a soup pot. Add the water, boil, then simmer for a couple hours. Strain into a container and discard the vegetables.

And there you have it: pure potassium broth, ready to freeze or keep fresh for about five days in the refrigerator. Eat it while fasting, or simply as a high-alkaline supplement to your diet.

---

[1]   A widely published scientist and researcher, Barry Sears is president of the biotechnology firm Eicotech and is the bestselling author of The Zone books. http://www.amazon.com/Zone-Revolutionary-Balance-Permanent-Weight ebook/dp/B000FC2P60/ref=sr_1_1?ie=UTF8&qid=1399 138647&sr=8-1&keywords=enter+the+zone

[2]   John Douillard D.C. is an Ayurvedic physician, writer, professor, and chiropractor specializing in sports medicine.   http://www.amazon.com/3-Season-Diet-Nature-Intended-Cravings-ebook/dp/B000XUDGU8/ref=sr_1_1?s=books&ie=UTF 8&qid=1399138706&sr=1-1&keywords=three+season+diet

[3]   Paula Garbourg (1907 – 2004), was the founder and developer of the Ring Muscle Method. The system she developed over years of research in Israel is based on the body's natural ability to heal itself. Garbourg determined that the various ring muscles function as one system, mutually connected to all bodily systems. http://paula.org.il/zope/home/en/1/about_principles_en/

[4]   "Most people know that sugar is not good for them," reports Kristin Kirkpatrick in the *Huffpost Healthy Living* blog, "but for some reason they think the risk of excess sugar

consumption is less than that of having too much saturated and trans fat, sodium, or calories." http://www.huffingtonpost.com/kristin-kirkpatrick-ms-rd-ld/dangers-of-sugar_b_3658061.html

5   Stevia grows best in warm conditions similar to those preferred by basil according to Barbara Pleasant in the Feb/March 2013 *Mother Earth News.* http://www.motherearthnews.com/organic-gardening/stevia-plant-zm0z13fmzkin.aspx#axzz3AI3xwABp

12

Less is More

He who takes medicine and neglects to diet wastes the skill of his doctors.
—CHINESE PROVERB

What if... scientists announced the discovery of a simple, provable method for extending the human life span?

What if... that method were so uncomplicated and inexpensive that it was available to everyone?

What if... despite the evidence, people rejected the method and continued to shorten their normal life spans?

None of this is conjecture. Science *has* come up with such a method. The even better news is that the method *is* available to everyone. The bad news is that it is being largely ignored by most of the developed world.

This simple approach to a longer, better life is calorie reduction. In layman's terms, it means eating less, but not just for the obvious reasons of weight control and elimination of diseases attributed to overeating. The benefits of calorie restricted diets have been known for many years. Dr. Roy Walford, a pioneer in longevity research, argued in his 1986 book, *The 120 Year Diet,* that the human life span can be significantly increased by a diet containing all the required nutrients—*but a third fewer calories.* Walford backed up his argument with *The Anti-Aging Plan* in which he offered a regimen of daily high-nutrition menus containing fewer than 1,500 calories per day.

Since Walford's work there have been innumerable studies on various species of animals, including humans, with differing rates of metabolism. The evidence suggests that the human body "wears out" after having processed something around seventy million calories. Burning those calories at a rate of 1,500 per day works out to a life span of about—ready for this?—*127 years*. If true, it means Walford's far-out guess of a 110 to a 120 year life span is not farfetched.[1] So why *aren't* we living that long? Why is the life expectancy in the U.S.—where we spend more than *any* nation on health care—only about seventy-eight years?

One huge reason: Americans eat too much. The gloomy truth is—if Walford's theory about total calories processed is correct—they use up their calories too soon.

Of course the science of longevity and calorie intake is far more complex than the simple burn rate of calories, but the underlying message seems clear. Eat less, live longer. And not just longer, but more productively. Gain joy not from eating but by accomplishing worthwhile missions.

Calorie restriction may deliver greater benefits than just living longer and being slimmer. A study in the *Journal of the Federation of American Societies' Experimental Biology* concluded that calorie reduction also protects brain cells from aging and improves brain function. In the study, scientists fed a test group of rats an unrestricted diet. Another group was fed a diet with 40% fewer calories. The subjects on the unrestricted diet showed a 60% decrease in a protein called Sirtuin 1 (SIRT 1) that protects brain cells from degeneration, while the calorie-restricted rats experienced an *increase* in the protective protein and a decrease in DNA fragmentation (a good indicator of cell death).

Does this mean a calorie-restricted diet may be a factor in prolonging *your* cognitive powers also? The evidence is promising. While the research in neurodegeneration and its link to diet is still ongoing, the benefits of calorie restriction seem too clear to ignore.

But how do you restrict your total calorie intake without starving yourself? Without being perpetually hungry? Without being anorexic?

One method is the ancient art of fasting—or a modified version of it. While the object of fasting has varied—curing illness,

rejuvenation, religious observance, cleansing and strengthening—
the net effect has always been the same: calorie restriction.

Here are some of the benefits of fasting:

Promotes weight loss.
Normalizes hunger hormone levels
Reduces oxidative stress.
Balances insulin and leptin sensitivity.
Boosts mitochondrial energy efficiency.
   Resets the body to use fat as its primary fuel. New research shows that when the body adapts to using fat instead of sugar, your risk of chronic disease is dramatically reduced.
Promotes human growth hormone (HGH) production.
Lowers triglyceride levels.
   Promotes cognitive vitality. Burning fat produces ketones (not glucose), a healthier fuel for your brain.
   Fasting increases production of the brain-derived neurotrophic factor (BDNF), which activates brain stem cells to convert into new neurons, and triggers numerous other chemicals that promote neural health. This protects brain cells from changes associated with Alzheimer's and Parkinson's disease as well.

Fasting should be easy and nurturing. It can range from a day to a week or more. If the very idea of fasting seems too extreme or impractical, then you can obtain the same calorie-restricted benefits by following an eating schedule that includes full meals on some days and dramatically cuts calories on others.

One method is to fast between regular meals, omitting all snacks, eating only on an empty stomach. Leave at least four hours between meals. Or simply skip the evening meal, substituting a light snack, a cup of milk, or *lassi* (two heaping tablespoons of yoghurt with a teaspoon of honey mixed in boiling water).

Another popular method is the 5:2 plan. You follow a normal meal schedule five days a week and fast for two. During fasting days, if you choose, you can still eat as much as 600 calories on fasting days. As on all fasting days, drink plenty of water and tea. According to nutritionists, the best way to stick to such a schedule is by having a light breakfast, taking most of your calories at lunch, omitting dinner.

An even simpler variation is alternate day fasting—eating one day, skipping the next. If such a schedule causes sleeping problems, try a *lassi* or hot milk at bed time.

Whichever routine you choose to follow, the objective is the same: a calorie-reduced diet. Eat less, enjoy life more.

---

[1] Walford wrote that following his calorie-restricted diet means "you are holding something like four aces in the poker game with Death." Ironically, though Walford considered himself one of his test subjects, he never made it to triple digits. He died at age seventy-nine of amyotrophic lateral sclerosis, or Lou Gehrig's disease. Since Walford's death, critics and advocates of Walford's work have argued about what role, if any, his diet may have played in his death.

13

The Power of Posture

Never slouch, as doing so compresses the lungs, overcrowds other vital organs, rounds the back, and throws you off balance.
—JOSEPH H. PILATES

Imagine this scene. You're at a cocktail party. You're in a large room, and you see the other guests standing in clusters, drinking and chatting. Across the floor, silhouetted against the sun-filled verandah, is a group you don't recognize. In the glare of the sun you can't see faces, just the profiles.

Now guess the ages of each person in the group. See the man whose head slants forward at a forty-five degree angle from his slumping shoulders? He looks... what? Seventy-something? Perhaps older. See the slender woman with the chin-up, head-back, spine-straight posture, one hand parked on her hip? Even in silhouette, she looks young. By that poised stance you guess that she could be a model. Notice the sway-backed man with the jutting head and mid-section? Definitely of upper Social Security vintage.

These are only guesses, and you might be close. And you might be dead wrong. The man with the outward-angling head is a fifty-year-old who looks like he's eighty. And the svelte model with the runway carriage? She turns out to be a woman in her seventies who has the posture of a teenager. The sway-backed man who appears to belong in assisted living? Forty-something going on seventy.

The point of this exercise? Looking young—or old—is an attitude. How you stand, how you carry yourself, how you appear to others is a reflection of how you think about yourself. Whether you are ebullient, depressed, curious, or bored is revealed in your posture. Conversely, your posture affects how you think about yourself. Your posture has a direct link to your state of mind.

Glance again at those people across the room. Those judgments you made about them reflected not only *your* view of them, it mirrored *their* view of themselves. The slouching, slump-shouldered man is habitually negative in his outlook. Life has beaten him down. The seventy-something woman has an upbeat, eager view of her world. It shows in her confident, upright stance.

Our thinking about posture is ingrained in our language. We associate "slouch" with someone who is weak or irresponsible in their task. The expression "chin up" is not only a morale-booster, it can be taken as good advice about posture.

Poor posture, particularly in senior adults, causes joint pain, breathing problems, difficulty walking, and contributes to falls by elderly people. Sitting at a desk or in a vehicle for long hours is where you get into the most postural trouble. Focusing on a computer screen causes the head to tilt forward. The body follows the head, and the thoracic and lumbar spine tends to round forward as well. Over time this leads to anatomical changes—postural muscles becoming imbalanced, making it progressively more difficult to stand up straight. Other problems include constricted nerves and blood vessels, muscle pain, and spinal maladjustment.

But you already know that, don't you? Or, at least, you've been hearing it all your life, beginning with your mother's admonition to stand up straight. She was right, but what she didn't tell you was that your slouching stance not only messes with your musculoskeletal system, it affects your emotional health. Just as bad posture has ramifications in your physical well being, an erect, confident posture translates to a more positive, vibrant attitude.

In a highly acclaimed TED talk, [1] Harvard professor and researcher Amy Cuddy sparked a sensation by offering a free, low-tech hack. Cuddy prescribes a "power pose"—an upright, open, confident stance—for just 120 seconds. Her studies show that this two-minute exercise has the immediate effect of lowering cortisol, the stress-related hormone, and elevating testosterone, creating not only a positive impact on how you're perceived by others but how you see yourself. "Your body language shapes who you are," says Dr. Cuddy. "Change your posture for two minutes . . . It could significantly change the way your life unfolds."

Here are examples of low-power, low-confidence poses: a slouching stance, a protective gesture such as placing your hand on your face or neck, hiding your hands in your pockets. All these poses suggest to other people—and to yourself—that you lack confidence and assertiveness. Strong poses—the kind Cuddy suggests in her two-minute hack—include the "Superman/Wonder Woman" pose, making yourself appear bigger, feet apart, hands on hips (the cape is optional). During your two-minute session, hold your arms up in a V-shape and lift your chin as if you'd just triumphed in an Olympic dash. The effect will be to make you feel—and appear—more powerful and confident.

If the secret to a more powerful and confident attitude is as simple as changing your posture, why isn't everyone standing tall and proud? One reason is that the ergonomics of our daily lives discourage holding a more erect pose. Psychotherapist Donna Ray says, "One of the things that happen with people in our day and age is that we tend to gaze downward because of the demands of our busy culture. People are looking down at their computer and phone screens. They're also looking down at the sidewalk, to make sure they don't trip—or because they don't want to look into the eyes of other people who are walking around them. Looking at birds and the sky actually activates back muscles for upright posture, and that makes people feel immediately better because it makes them feel more alert."

You weren't born with poor posture. Instead, you trained for it, and improving your posture requires changing years of ingrained habits. Here are some ways to work toward an improved posture:

— **Analyze your posture.**

Have photos taken of you from three angles—side, front, behind. Look for imbalances. Are your head and neck centered over your body? Is one arm or hip lower than the other? Pay attention to correcting any imbalances in your posture. A free app for the iPhone and iPad called PostureZone overlays your photos against a grid and assesses your posture.

— **Take frequent breaks from your work station.**

Stand up, walk around, stretch. Take a few minutes to perform light exercise, throw darts, juggle. These activities refresh your body as well as your brain.

— **Stand with your shoulder blades pulled back.**

Imagine capturing a pencil between your shoulder blades. This activates the rhomboid and middle trapezius muscles, which are weak in most of the adult population.[2] Isometrically contract your abdominal muscles by sucking the belly button inward toward the spine, contracting your core muscles.

— **Work at an upright desk.**

Consider using a work surface at which you can alternate sitting and standing up. You can install an inexpensive draftsman's table, or a simple lectern, or invest in a height-adjustable platform like the GeekDesk or the Varidesk, which fits atop a regular work surface.

— **Observe yourself.**

Make random observations about your posture and correlate them to how you feel at the moment. Try adjusting your posture and note how it affects your attitude. Jot the observations in your notebook. Review your notebook entries to see if a pattern emerges.

— Improve your balance

Your posture is directly related to your ability to balance. Strengthening your balance promotes a strong posture, and, conversely, an upright, aligned posture strengthens your balance.

And *how*, you ask, do you improve your balance? Easy. Like this:

Balance of Power

Around the age of forty, you begin to experience a subtle deterioration in your balance. This has ramifications in all aspects of your physical—and even mental—efficiency. Your ability to balance has a direct connection to performance in strength training, endurance sports, and on your overall health.

Age isn't the only factor that affects your balance. Balance is thrown off by weakened eyesight, inflexible muscles, alcohol, and medications like antidepressants, blood pressure drugs, and sleep medicines. For senior adults, shaky balance can be the beginning of a downward spiral. Fearful of falling, they cut back on physical activities, causing essential muscles to weaken, which makes them even *more* unsteady and sets them up for a deadly spill.[3]

The good news is that balance, like muscle mass, is restorable. In fact it becomes increasingly vital for senior adults to maintain not only their general fitness but also their ability to balance.

Regaining and reinforcing your sense of balance can be a hugely rewarding mission in your pursuit of Mastery. Make balancing on one leg a routine exercise. Even better, insert one-legged balancing into your daily life—standing in line, drying off after a shower, taking a break from your desk—and can be included in resistance-training exercises.

Here are some drills to train your vestibular system, the mechanism in your inner ear that alerts you to impending upsets and serves as your orienting tool. These exercises stimulate this underused sense, making you more responsive to the tiny deviations in your balancing act.

— *Weight shifts.*

Stand with your feet apart with your weight on both legs. Shift your weight to one side and lift the other foot off the floor. Hold the position as long as you can without wobbling. Shoot for 30 seconds. Repeat the drill on the other leg. As you get better (and you will), increase the length of each repetition.

— *Single-leg stance.*

Again stand with feet apart, hands on your hips, weight equally distributed. Lift one leg and bend it back at the knee. Hold the position for 30 seconds, then return to the starting position and repeat with the other leg. When you can do this without excessive wobbling, throw in some movements with the free leg. Hold your foot out as far as possible. Bend your knee and rotate it as far as you can in each direction. Lean forward and touch the ground while keeping your free leg extended. When this becomes easy, perform the drill on an unstable surface like a pillow. The best part about this drill is that it can be almost anywhere—drying off after a shower, standing in grocery checkout lines, airport security mazes, waiting for a subway. Ignore the stares. You know something they don't.

— *Balancing with the eyes closed.*

Take it to the next level. Start with your feet together, eyes closed, and slowly raise yourself onto the balls of your feet. Without visual clues, your vestibular system goes into high gear. You can feel the tiny muscles in your feet, ankles, and calves working overtime to keep you balanced. When you become reasonably stable in this position, return to a flat-footed stance, close the eyes and stand on one leg. At first it may seem impossible, but with practice it will come. And then balancing on one leg, eyes open, will be a walk in the park.

— *Single-leg balancing during upper body exercises.*

Here's a two-for-one. Incorporate your new one-legged skill into another exercise. Try doing slow bicep curls with a light dumbbell while standing on one leg on the same side. When you can do half a dozen reps this way, switch to curling with one arm while standing on the opposite leg. Using the same technique, you can perform shoulder presses—vertical raises with a light dumbbell—again balanced on one leg. Try side-lateral raises—holding a light dumbbell at your side and lifting it slowly until your arm is perpendicular to the floor—on one leg. Be imaginative. Defy gravity.

— *Tandem walking.*

Place your feet as if you were walking on a tight rope or the narrow edge of a plank. Place one foot in front of the other, heel of the leading foot touching the toe of the trailing foot. Then position the trailing foot in front, heel touching toe. Practice this until it becomes natural. Take it outdoors. Look for opportunities to tandem walk on narrow curbs, lines on sidewalks, fallen logs. Be a kid again. Ignore the curious stares.

As with every mission in Mastery, physical and mental, establish goals. Don't be satisfied just to be able to perform an exercise, or to have devoted a specific amount of time to an objective. Determine a goal, then measure your progress toward it. Better yet, include the goal in a broader mission. This is a core principle of Mastery.

---

[1]   In her TED talk, Amy Cuddy told her audience, "Tiny tweaks can lead to big changes. So this is two minutes. Two minutes, two minutes, two minutes. Before you go into the next stressful evaluative situation, for two minutes, try doing this, in the elevator, in a bathroom stall, at your desk behind closed doors. That's what you want to do. Configure your brain to cope the best in that situation. Get your testosterone up. Get your cortisol down. Don't leave that situation feeling like, oh, I didn't show them who I am. Leave that situation feeling like, oh, I really feel like I got to say who I am and show who I am." http://www.ted.com/talks/amy_cuddy_your_body_langu age_shapes_who_you_are?language=en

[2]   Ken Baldwin, executive director of the National Posture Institute and professor at the State University of New York, says, "You need to think about your posture every thirty minutes you are awake." http://www.refinery29.com/2013/08/51619/posture.

[3]   "Regardless of your age, if you can't stand steadily on one leg for at least 15 seconds — with or without your eyes closed — then you definitely need to start practicing as soon as possible to improve your balance," says Dr. John Morley, gerontologist and author of *The Science of Staying Young*.

14

Sleep

Finish each day before you begin the next, and interpose a solid wall of sleep between the two.
—RALPH WALDO EMERSON

You remember it well. You have pleasant memories of that time in your life, not so long ago, when you could sleep. *Really* sleep. You could sleep so deeply you felt that you were in another universe. It was the kind of sleep that began minutes after your head hit the pillow. You slept straight through the night and awoke with a wide-eyed, energized feeling, knowing you could take on whatever life had to throw at you. Sleep was your friend, your fuel, your personal rejuvenator.

And then something happened. In small increments, the quality of sleep changed. Instead of being a joy, sleep became a necessary drudgery, neither pleasant nor restorative. These days you have trouble going to sleep, or you have trouble staying asleep, or you wake multiple times at night while your mind rambles like a deranged monkey. Sometimes you linger in bed hoping for sleep, or else you just suck it up and get on with your day.

You yearn for a good night's sleep. Even more, you yearn for that magical, bright-eyed feeling it used to produce.

Is the feeling gone forever? Or is it possible for you to recapture some of that lost ability, just as you can recapture other faculties that have eroded over the years? The answer is. . .

You *can* regain the ability to sleep well. And you can do it the same way you regain any cognitive or physical ability (sleeping involves both) as you accomplish missions in Mastery—by conscious application.

As a first step in learning how to improve your sleep, you must determine *why* you don't sleep well. There are usually multiple reasons, some valid, some mythical.

Myth: *You need less sleep as you age.*
Truth: *Older adults require seven to eight hours of sleep every night—pretty much what they always needed.*

Even if you believe the myth about needing less sleep, your body definitely does not. When your sleep is repeatedly cut short night after night, you feel it in a lack of vitality and an ongoing tiredness. The cumulative effect of sleep deprivation has serious consequences for your health and well-being.

If you've been getting by on insufficient sleep, you're paying the price in reduced energy and productivity. Your motivation is reduced. Your mission effectiveness suffers.

Okay, you need as much sleep as ever. But doesn't aging affect your *ability* to sleep? Yes, but not in the way you may think. Simply growing older isn't the main culprit in the loss of sleep quality. As you age and mature, your circadian rhythm gradually changes. Each phase of your life, from infancy to adolescence to mature adulthood, has its own unique sleep rhythms. Your internal biological clock that regulates the windows of wakefulness and sleepiness makes subtle shifts as you grow older. The window during which your internal clock enables sleep narrows, which is why you may find yourself waking earlier in the morning and falling asleep earlier in the evening.

Does this mean that beyond a certain age you will no longer be able to sleep well? That quality sleep is a distant memory? Not at all. What it means is that you have to adjust your approach to sleep to accommodate what we call evolving reality. Just as you have to adjust the intensity of weight workouts or running sessions to match your physiology, so must you change sleep habits.

Aging isn't the only factor that affects the ability to sleep. Illnesses, medications, life transitions, hormonal changes, and ingrained bad habits can make quality sleep almost impossible. If despite your best efforts your sleep shows no improvement, it is possible that you have a disorder that requires professional diagnosis. Consider consulting a sleep center and doctor. Sleep disorders such as sleep apnea are insidious and can be deadly if not diagnosed.

How do you go about improving the quality of your sleep? By applying the principles of Mastery. By making it your mission to improve that third of your life you spend sleeping—or *trying* to sleep.

And just as you do before embarking on any mission, first get the facts:

The biology of Sleep

Your normal sleep cycle consists of two basic states—rapid eye movement (REM) sleep and non-rapid eye movement (NREM). In NREM sleep, you pass through four stages of brainwave activity before you reach REM sleep, then the cycle repeats. Each stage usually lasts five to fifteen minutes. In a normal night's sleep, you pass through the stages of NREM and REM sleep every 90-110 minutes.

— *Stage One:* The falling asleep phase, when you're drifting in and out of sleep and wake up easily. This is the stage when your muscles may contract suddenly and you have a sensation of falling.

— *Stage Two:* Eye movement stops and brain wave activity slows down with only an occasional burst of rapid brain waves. Adults spend nearly half their sleeping time in this stage.

— *Stages Three and Four:* The extremely slow brain waves called Delta take over. These two stages are called deep sleep—or delta sleep—with stage four being more intense than stage three.

There is no eye movement or muscle activity in these stages, and this is when it is most difficult to awaken you.

— *REM sleep:* You enter the REM state about ninety minutes after going to sleep. Your breathing becomes more irregular and shallow, your eyes jerk rapidly and your arm and leg muscles may be rigid. Most of your dreaming takes place in REM stage, and if you awake during REM sleep you probably remember your dream. (More on dreaming and dream recall later). Adults may spend as much as twenty percent of their sleep time in REM, though your time in REM sleep tapers down as you age.

Track Your Sleep

One of the basic steps in any mission is recording your progress. And so it is with sleep. In order to measure improvement in the quality of your sleep, you need to know *how* you're sleeping. But sleep can be a tough activity to track. With the exception of your go-to-bed and wake up times, patterns of light and deep and REM sleep can be difficult to measure unless you check into a specialized sleep clinic with hook ups to measure brain wave activity, eye movement analysis, and muscle tone evaluation.

Or at least that was the case until recently. A plethora of gadgets and apps have appeared that not only record your sleep patterns but offer analysis and input about how to improve. The list of devices and apps is changing rapidly as the technology evolves.

Here are a few of the better known devices currently on the market:

> — Basis Peak: The Peak not only measures movement, it also measures heart rate, skin temperature, and perspiration. From these data the device delivers statistics about your sleep and various sleep stages.

— Jawbone UP: One version of this device plugs into your iPhone, and another synchs via Bluetooth. The UP tracks and syncs all of your activity and sleep data. A button at the end of the bracelet is pressed to indicate sleep start and sleep stop. Jawbone comes with a "Today I Will" feature that allows you to set goals. The Jawbone head of data, Monica Rogati, says that people who use the feature have been 26% more likely to get seven to eight hours of sleep than those who don't set goals.

— FitBit: A series of popular wristband devices that track steps, distance, and sleep and comes with an effortless wireless interface to present daily data.

Apps to track your sleep.

— 24/7: An app available from the iTunes store that utilizes the actigraphy technology in your iTouch or smart phone and uses it to track sleep. While you can place the device on the bed, it is suggested that it be affixed to your arm for greater accuracy. Once you hit the sack, you just switch it into sleep mode.

— Sleep Cycle Alarm Clock: For iPhone and Android devices, this app graphs your sleep quality and lets you add sleep notes. Its alarm clock function can also wake you at your lightest sleep time using a soothing tone.

— SleepBot: Another popular app, SleepBot uses your phone's motion tracking feature to determine when you're getting the most and least amount of rest.

The business of sleep tracking is an emerging technology. New devices and apps keep coming out that purport to track your sleep patterns. Some work better than others. Since all these devices are *data collectors*, their value depends on what you do with the data.

Is improving your sleep a worthy mission? Absolutely. As with any mission, make sure you record the data you collect in a journal. Your sleep journal can also serve as a log for your dreams—a document guaranteed to be entertaining reading.

Retraining Your Brain to Sleep

The different bandwidths of your consciousness include beta—the waking state, and the alpha, theta, and delta frequencies—mostly sleeping states. Lying in bed waiting to fall asleep, you're still in beta, waiting for your brain to switch bandwidths. If you spend an unduly long time before falling asleep, it may be because your brain has become conditioned to *not* making the transition to the slow-wave sleeping bandwidths.

Why does your brain behave this way? Here's a theory advanced by personal development coach Steve Pavlina: By following an unstructured sleep schedule—going to bed and ruminating about whatever enters your mind while you wait to fall asleep, perhaps waking up and ruminating some more, then staying in bed too long trying to recapture lost sleep—you've made your brain lazy. Your subconscious mind has been conditioned to believe that there is no reason to go to sleep *now*, that your time in bed can be squandered. You believe the time you have to sleep is unlimited.[1]

It's a problem all too familiar to retirees who no longer have the built-in sleep discipline of their working life. Their brains have become de-incentivized to making efficient use of sleep time.

The solution? Re-incentivize your brain. Retrain it to cease all that wasteful ruminating and make the transition *now* into sleep mode. Train your brain that oversleeping is not an option. You will adjust to the notion that sleep time is a limited resource, and going to sleep faster is the way to optimize that resource.

The first step in the retraining process is to use an alarm clock. Pick a wake up time and stick to it. Waking up at a specific time every day and exiting the bed *immediately* reinforces the message to your brain that your time in bed is finite.

Won't this, at least at first, leave you groggy, perhaps sleep-deprived? Possibly. And that's why taking a nap—or naps—is a great idea. But—and this is important—limit each nap to *twenty minutes*. No more, and not later than mid-afternoon so as not to impact your ability to go to sleep at night. Again, use an alarm clock. The timer or alarm on your smart phone works great for this purpose. Be strict. Make yourself get up immediately when the alarm sounds. Whether you actually sleep or not is less important than that you implant this message in your subconscious: *This is all the time I have to sleep. Make the most of it.*

The retraining process may take a while, especially if your sleep habits have become unstructured over a period of years. The naps are important, not just to reinforce the message that sleep time is limited, but to actually make up for lost sleep during the night.

Again, for the process to work, you have to be disciplined. No lingering in bed after the alarm either in the morning or following your naps. Your foggy brain is a seductive rationalizer when you're just waking up: *Another half hour in bed is all I need . . . what's the big deal about getting up so early . . . just this one time I can sleep in . . .*

And while you're retraining your brain, put all the other sleep improvement tools to work. Some will work for you, others may not. None have serious downsides. Go ahead and experiment. Take control of your body—and of your sleep.

Sleep Hacks

Here are a few techniques and gadgets, some of them deceptively simple, that have been shown to enhance sleep quality.

Sleep Hack #1: *Stick a foot, or two feet, outside the covers.* To which you may say, *Wait a minute.* Isn't this something you've been doing all your life? Sure, but not necessarily to make yourself sleepy. Before you fall asleep, your body temperature begins to drop. In the deepest stage of sleep, the temperature is at its lowest, a couple degrees below normal. This is why taking a warm bath or drinking a warm liquid just before going to bed makes you sleepy. Your body temperature is cooling rapidly, which induces slumber.

Which is why sticking your foot out works. Your feet and hands are natural dissipaters of body heat, and the uncovered foot induces the temperature drop in your body that precedes sleep.

Sleep Hack #2: *Light therapy.* Used for SAD (seasonal affective disorder) and jet lag sufferers, light-emitting devices have also been shown to help regulate the sleeping/waking rhythm. Users of devices like the <u>Philips goLITE</u>, a blue light emitting device the size of a small pocketbook, report getting to sleep in much shorter time after using the device for brief sessions during the day. Using the goLITE first thing in the morning reportedly quickens the wake up process and tops off your energy level. During the work day you park the light at your desk or work table so that it shines tangentially on your face for about fifteen minutes. According to proponents, the goLITE helps regulate serotonin and melatonin levels, hormones essential to the sleeping/waking rhythm of your body.

Another blue light-emitting device is the Nightwave, a box about the size of a cigarette pack that projects a soft blue light into your darkened bedroom. The luminance of the light slowly rises and falls, and you synchronize your breathing with the waves of light. Your focus on the external cue of the light produces a deep relaxation that leads to natural sleep.

Sleep Hack #3: *Control your environment.* Remember the old adage that says that the bedroom should be used *only* for sleep or for sex? Believe it. For better sleep, don't let your bedroom serve as a workplace, theatre, reading room, pet sanctuary, or eating nook. The light from glowing screens—television, computer, digital tablets—pass through the retina and have the effect of delaying the onset of sleep. Worse, mental engagement with television or email or any activity that stimulates your brain also impacts your sleep.[2] Keep your bedroom dark, quiet, and cool. Use light blocking curtains or shades. Try a sleeping mask and ear plugs to block out unwanted light and outside noises.. The ideal sleeping temperature for most people is somewhere between 65—70 degrees. Dissipating your body heat induces sleep, which is why the sticking-one-foot-out hack also works.

Sleep Hack #4: *Aromatherapy.* The sense of smell is a powerful stimulant to your mental state. Certain essential oils have long been used to promote relaxation and natural sleep. Among them, Lavender is recognized as the best sleep aid, though some people prefer Orange or Roman Chamomile. All have nurturing effects and serve as natural tranquilizers.

Essential oils can be used in several ways for sleep therapy. Apply it as a mist on your head, face, back of your neck, and pillow. Or place a drop of the oil on a cotton ball under your pillow. Oils like Lavender are good in a warm bath before bed time, inducing a naturally drowsy, ready-to-sleep state. A good source for information and for individualized essential oil blends is <u>Oil Lady Aromatherapy</u>.

Sleep Hack #5: *Exercise*. This, too, may seem obvious. Haven't you always known that exercise has a direct effect in getting a good night's sleep? Yes, but the effect is in the timing. Remember the correlation between body temperature and the onset of sleep? Half an hour or so of aerobic exercise raises your body temperature and stimulates your brain and muscles for several hours, which seriously interferes with sleep. The sweet spot for vigorous exercise is a late afternoon or early evening session, *at least three hours before bedtime*. Your raised body temperature will begin decreasing just as you're ready for bed, triggering the onset of sleep.

How important is improving your sleep? You devote a third of your life to this activity. Given the potential dividends in increased energy and productivity, improving the quality of your sleep could be one of the most rewarding missions you ever pursue.

---

[1] In his blog post, *How to Fall Asleep in Less Than 30 Seconds*, Steve Pavlina maintains that your brain can be trained to

go to sleep quickly and you can stop squandering time in bed. "When you go to bed whenever and allow yourself to get up whenever, you reward your brain for continued laziness and inefficiency. It's fine if you take a half hour to fall asleep since your brain knows it can just sleep in later. If you awaken with an alarm but go to bed earlier than necessary to compensate for the time it takes you to fall asleep, you still tell your brain that it's fine to waste time transitioning to sleep because there's still enough extra time to get the rest it needs." http://www.stevepavlina.com/blog/2013/07/how-to-fall-asleep-in-less-than-30-seconds/

[2] According to Mark Rosekind, PhD, former director of the Fatigue Countermeasures Program at the NASA Ames Research Center, "As your brain revs up, its electrical activity increases and neurons start to race -- the exact opposite of what should be happening before sleep. A second reason has to do with your body: The physical act of responding to a video game or even an email makes your body tense. As you get stressed, your body can go into a 'fight or flight' response, and as a result, cortisol, a stress hormone produced by the adrenal gland, is released, creating a situation hardly conducive to sleep." http://www.webmd.com/sleep-disorders/features/power-down-better-sleep

Part Four

Powers of Mind

There is nothing either good or bad, but thinking makes it so.
—WILLIAM SHAKESPEARE

ROBERT GANDT AND GARY A. SCOTT

15

The Fast Way to Slow Down

Meditation is to dive all the way within, beyond thought, to the source of thought and pure consciousness. It enlarges the container, every time you transcend. When you come out, you come out refreshed, filled with energy and enthusiasm for life.
— DAVID LYNCH

It happens. You've undertaken a challenging mission, making progress on your goals, then you hit a rough patch. Your focus wavers. Self-doubt creeps like a dank fog into your consciousness. You're going as fast as you can, and your brain is screaming at you to go faster.

Question: *What do you do?*

Answer: *Slow down. Way down.*

Does this seem counterintuitive? It's not, and here's why.

During most of your waking life your brain is engaged in a fast-track monologue during which every thought, every emotional link, triggers another thought. Then another. All day long your brain spins these thoughts about your work, your family, your finances, your mission.

Much of this spin is negative. It flows from what neuroscientists call your *negativity bias*, a survival instinct handed down from your Paleolithic ancestors whose attention was focused more on looming threats than on positive rewards. And correctly so, considering their exposure to predators and natural calamities. Like it or not, the fight-or-flight instinct is embedded in your genes—and it has a direct connection to modern day stress, anxiety, and depression.

But you're not a Paleolithic human. So how do you slow down while your mind is raging against the latest stressful event in your life?

You meditate.

And at this point you may be forgiven for saying... *whaaaat?* You might be among those who think that meditation is some form of eastern ritual practiced by monks, hippies, and incense burners, but not by otherwise normal, productive, western-oriented people like yourself. No way. It doesn't fit your rational persona.

Think again.

It is estimated that somewhere near twenty million people in the U.S. practice meditation, and the number is swelling. Meditation is becoming one of the most-used therapies for stress reduction, healing, and problem solving. In recent years there has been an explosion of scientific data on the effects of meditation, much of it from studies using functional magnetic resonance imaging (fMRI) equipment to measure subjects' responses to stimuli before, during, and after meditation.[1]

Phil Jackson, coach of the Los Angeles Lakers, has his team meditating. Corporations like General Mills, Facebook, and Target have their employees doing meditation. U.S. Congressmen, including Rep. Tim Ryan, practice meditation. "It's a quiet revolution that's happening," Ryan told *CBS Evening News.* "I think at some point the more we understand about how the brain works, the more this is going to catch on."[2]

Meditation has been shown to—

— Enhance creativity
— Expand memory
— Increase rate of learning
— Reduce anxiety
— Help develop a more positive outlook
— Strengthen the immune system

— Promote better and deeper sleep
— Increase vitality
— Lower blood pressure
— Help resolve addictions

What really happens when you meditate? One of the most significant results is that your brain stops its frenetic processing of information. That fast track dialogue spinning through your mind all day long slows to a whisper. A marvelous effect called *neuroplasticity*—the change of brain structure as a result of experience—goes to work. A collection of independent studies [3] using Magnetic Resonance Imaging on control groups of meditators and non-meditators found distinct changes in the brain structures of those who regularly practiced meditation.

The changes they identified in the meditators' brains included:

— Increased cortical thickness (area of the brain associated with attention and sensory processing).
— Increased gray matter density in the brain stem (associated with mechanisms of cardiorespiratory control).
— Increased gray matter in the left hippocampus (brain area involved in learning and memory)

While the notion of actually altering the structure of your brain by meditating may seem strange, science confirms that your brain possesses the ability to change its own wiring. Meditation stimulates new and different neurotransmitters, builds circuits, and enlarges shrinking brain centers.

Meditation Techniques

Most methods of meditation involve concentration, relaxation, open awareness techniques, or a combination of these. Besides the traditional sitting posture, meditation can also be done walking, standing, or lying down (many people simply fall asleep while meditating in a prone position). Each is a means of cultivating a calm and clear state of mind.

Here is an overview of the most commonly used forms of meditation.

Concentrative Meditation

A broad term to include those meditation techniques that focus attention on some object. The object can be your breath, an image, a flame, a sound. By consistently returning your attention to the object of focus, the mind gradually attains a state of calm.

Transcendental Meditation

TM is a trademarked form of concentrative meditation based on the use of a mantra, a calming word or phrase. Sitting in a comfortable position with your eyes closed, you silently repeat the mantra, usually a word or sound from the Vedic tradition that has been chosen for you. While meditating and mentally repeating the mantra, your ordinary thinking process is "transcended," and you enter a state of calm and pure consciousness.

Mindfulness

Considered a passive form of meditation, "Mindfulness" means being aware of your thoughts, feelings, bodily sensations, your surrounding environment in the present moment, without applying judgment. In recent years Mindfulness has become a favored technique in part through the work of Jon Kabat-Zinn and his Mindfulness-based-stress-reduction (MBSR) program, which he established at the University of Massachusetts Medical School.

As with most forms of meditation, a Mindfulness session begins by taking a comfortable sitting position on the floor or in a chair. Focus on the breath moving in and out of your body, feeling your belly rise and fall, paying attention to each individual breath and how it is different. Watch each thought as though you were an external observer, neither ignoring nor suppressing the thoughts, using your breath as an anchor.

Guided meditations

Most forms of meditation can be guided. A guided meditation is conducted by a guide's live voice or via a recording. The meditation may take the subject on a mental tour of a forest, ocean front, mountain path with appropriate background music or environmental sounds. Guided meditation CDs and MP3s are readily available and allow you to experience the meditation at a time and place of your choice. Guided meditations are especially useful in rehabilitation therapy following surgery or trauma, and are effective tools for rehearsing successful outcomes for performers and athletes.

Walking meditations

As with other forms of concentrative meditation, your attention during a walking meditation is focused on a single object—the physical experience of walking. The meditation is best done outdoors, along a quiet route, not combined with errands or exercise or any other distraction. While walking at a relaxed but normal pace, you pay attention to the sensations of your body.

Labyrinths

Labyrinth walking is a form of meditation that dates back over 4,000 years. A labyrinth is a man-made, spiral pattern path traced on the ground, often in a garden, in designs that range from decoration to ancient myth. Labyrinths are found in churchyards, parks, spa resorts, medical facilities, and many private gardens. [4] The meditation begins at the entry to the labyrinth. As you follow the circuitous route to the center, your focus, as with other walking meditations, remains on the physical sensation of walking. The symbolism of taking the journey can be used to resolve a problem, answer a question, or to reach a higher plane of thought.

Many labyrinth walkers choose to go barefoot, believing that the tactile stimulation allows closer contact with the earth's energy. The pace can be fast or slow with the mind focused on the feel of motion, the air, the heat, the feet, all the senses. The center of the labyrinth is the deepest point in the meditation walk. There you can pause, sit, and surrender totally to your inner process. The journey out of the labyrinth, according to devotees, is when insights and higher intelligence are experienced. The walk may be considered a metaphor for the journey to the center of your deepest self and out again into the world.

Meditation Basics

Dispense with the notion that meditation requires a special place, a certain pose such as the lotus position, or exotic background sounds like chants or eastern spiritual music. The truth is that once you've learned, you can meditate *anywhere at any time*. While many techniques of meditation were originally derived from philosophies and customs associated with religion (Hinduism, Buddhism), understand that all such associations are optional. Meditation requires only a willingness to focus your mind.

Here are some basics :

Avoid external distractions.

Turn off the TV, the smartphone, any device that may interrupt your concentration. You don't need music, and it may even be distracting at first. If you use sounds, make it something calm and repetitive. Or use a "white" noise—a recording of a seashore or gentle breeze or a fountain. With practice you'll learn to meditate despite outside noises like lawnmowers or barking dogs. You'll be aware of them without letting them dominate your thoughts.

Make yourself comfortable.

If you're a beginner, you'll probably want to take a sitting position. The traditional practice is to sit on a cushion on the floor or ground. Unless you're very flexible, crossing your legs in the lotus or half-lotus may be uncomfortable and distracting. Choose a posture on a comfortable chair or bench, with your pelvis tilted slightly forward and your spine supporting all your weight from the waist up. You can rest hands in the traditional palms-up position in your lap or relaxed at your sides. For a good overview of the best positions for meditation, check out the _Zen Mountain Monastery_ site.

Close your eyes.

It's best in the beginning to meditate with the eyes closed in order to block out external visual stimuli while you're calming your mind. Later you may find that you can meditate equally well with your eyes open, keeping them in "soft focus" mode.

Since it's virtually impossible to keep your mind an empty void, the key to meditation is to focus on a single object or a thought. While meditating you can focus on—

Breathing.

This is the most basic of meditation techniques and is the basis of mindfulness meditation. Let your mind dwell on a spot just above your navel and focus on the rise and fall of your abdomen as you breathe in and out. You become an observer, making no judgments or decisions about the number or quality of your breaths. When your mind wanders, simply observe the stray thought with acceptance, then calmly return your focus to your breathing. In the classic text about meditation and breathing, *The Miracle of Mindfulness,* Thich Nhat Hanh makes a strong case for how your breathing is connected to the mind, which controls the body. By focusing exclusively on one object—your breathing—you bring your entire being to a point of stillness.[5]

A Sound.

A common form of meditation is to silently repeat a mantra—a word or phrase—over and over until your mind becomes still and you enter a meditative state. In Sanskrit, mantra means "instrument of the mind." Pick any mantra you like, preferably one that invokes a mood of calm and peacefulness. Or choose a mantra that has a meaning within your own spiritual tradition. Good mantras might include words like *calm, tranquil, flow.*

A Visual Image

In this form of meditation you keep your eyes open, in "soft focus" mode, gazing at a simple object such as the flame of a candle, a flower, a picture or statue. Gaze at the object, keeping your eyes in "soft focus," until your peripheral vision closes in and the object consumes your entire focus. In the same way repeating a mantra stills your mind, concentrating on the flame or flower to the exclusion of all other stimuli will lead to you to a calm and serene meditative state.

An alternative visual mode of meditation is by focusing your mind on an imagined color, or a pattern of colors such as the colors of the rainbow. According to Hindu and/or Buddhist tradition, everyone has seven energy centers, called *chakras* in Sanskrit, each corresponding to a specific area of the body and a color. Focusing on one of these specific colors during meditation, practitioners believe, has the effect of "opening" the related chakra and thus freeing up mental and physical energy.

There is no single best way to meditate. It's not a skill you acquire immediately, but from day one you will see results. As in running, if you run, you're a runner, and if you meditate, you are a meditator. If you're just beginning, experiment until you determine which technique produces the most satisfying effect. For a small number of people, meditation may not seem to work at all. A number of others will find it just a pleasant way to relax and perhaps go to sleep. Most meditative disciplines suggest that if you stick to it without expectation, you will gain benefits even if you don't immediately recognize them.

Begin with short sessions. Pay attention to what works for you and what doesn't. For best results, try to meditate at least once a day, preferably twice. If you can, meditate first thing in the morning, and again at night. Consistency will produce the desired effect. Short meditations practiced regularly are more productive than long sessions infrequently.

Some meditations will feel wonderfully satisfying, some less so. Some days come easy and some not, but all produce beneficial results. As with all worthwhile endeavors, your best results come from effort, commitment, and reflection. Meditation is not only a powerful stress-reducer, it can be your secret weapon in the accomplishment of every mission.

MASTERY

1   Robert Piper, blogging in the *Huffington Post*, wrote, "Roughly 20 million Americans meditate; I'm not sure why the number isn't at least 80 million considering how great of a tool it is ... Running marathons is cool. Triathlons are cool. *Tough Mudder*—an event that hosts a 10-12 mile obstacle course that was designed by the British Special Forces—is cool. Lighting incense, closing your eyes, and listening to hippie music is currently not cool. I see possibly the greatest diamond in the rough being portrayed in popular culture the wrong way."

2   Congressman Tim Ryan grew up in a tough, beer-and-a-shot district in Youngstown, Ohio. Every morning in his living room he conducts a thirty-minute morning meditation, clearing his head of clutter. Ryan is the author of a book on meditation—A Mindful Nation: How a Simple Practice Can Help Us Reduce Stress, Improve Performance, and Recapture the American Spirit. During an interview with *CBS Evening News*, the congressman said the group that could benefit the most from meditation is his own— his colleagues in Washington. "I think if you look back at our country to the big mistakes that we made, it seems to me that we weren't seeing things quite clearly."

3   In one of the cited studies published in the Jan. 30, 2011 *Psychiatry Research: Neuroimaging*, Harvard neuroscientist Sara Lazar led a team of researchers to study the effect of meditation on the brain. In an eight-week program she and her team studied a group of sixteen subjects. Using Magnetic Resonance Imaging (MRI) during the subjects' meditations, the researchers observed a change in beta waves, indicating a decrease in information being processed the brain. The research

determined that specific areas of the brain were affected by meditation in different ways:

Frontal lobe: This is the most highly evolved part of the brain, responsible for reasoning, planning, emotions and self-conscious awareness. During meditation, the frontal cortex tends to go offline.

Parietal lobe: This part of the brain processes sensory information about the surrounding world, orienting you in time and space. During meditation, activity in the parietal lobe slows down.

Thalamus: The gatekeeper for the senses, this organ focuses your attention by funneling some sensory data deeper into the brain and stopping other signals in their tracks. Meditation reduces the flow of incoming information to a trickle.

Reticular formation: As the brain's sentry, this structure receives incoming stimuli and puts the brain on alert, ready to respond. Meditating dials back the arousal signal.

4   The Labyrinth Society and Veriditas have collaborated on a site called the World-Wide Labyrinth Locator at http://labyrinthlocator.com/. Go to the website and type in the town, state or country where you are searching. You can also pick a radius, such as "within 25 miles." A list of public labyrinths in churches, hospitals, parks, etc. with addresses will show up. There may be some private labyrinths on the list as well where the owners will allow people to walk if they call ahead.

5   "The instant you sit down to meditate," writes Nhat Hanh in *The Miracle of Mindfulness*, "begin watching your breath. At first breathe normally, gradually letting your

breathing slow down until it is quiet, even, and the lengths of the breaths are fairly long. From the moment you sit down to the moment your breathing has become deep and silent, be conscious of everything that is happening in yourself."

16

Muscle Memory

Repetitio mater studiorum est.
(LATIN PROVERB: *Repetition is the mother of learning*)

It's been forty years since Lowell Johnson flew a helicopter. Most of the technical jargon has been long forgotten—cyclic, collective, height/velocity envelopes. They are language from the long ago days when he was a young Army pilot in Vietnam.

And yet here he is, hands on the controls of this modern helicopter. And it all comes back. Somehow Johnson's hands and feet are maneuvering this complicated machine as if he had never left it.

What Lowell Johnson is experiencing is called muscle memory. It's the ability of your muscles to repeat a series of movements that you learned and then stored in your brain. When you catch a tossed ball, you're drawing on muscle memory. When you play a musical instrument you are repeating movements stored in muscle memory. When you ride a bicycle, your muscles are remembering lessons learned years ago. If you've ever flown helicopters, your muscles remember.

Muscle memory isn't actually stored in the muscles. Muscle memory resides in an area of your brain, deposited there like a cache of programmed instructions awaiting your summons. But muscle memory, as you'll see, can be strengthened like a muscle. Here's how.

Automaticity

Practice, the master of all things.
— Augustus Octavius

It is 1980. The crowd at the Lake Placid Olympics is going mad, yelling "USA! USA!" The U.S. ice hockey team, all amateur college kids, has just defeated the mighty Russian hockey team. American team coach Herb Brooks, wearing unfashionable plaid pants, is beside himself with joy. After scoring a third period goal that put them 4-3 over the Russians, the Americans battled on for another ten minutes to clinch their victory. The exuberant ABC announcer asks his audience a rhetorical question: "Do you believe in miracles?"

The mere suggestion—*miracles*—was enough to trigger a movement. Articles, testimonials, books poured forth, all gushing about the Olympic triumph. "Miracle on Ice" became a movie starring Kurt Russell.

In truth, the young Americans' victory had less to do with miracles than with the phenomenon called automaticity—the ultimate product of muscle memory. Automaticity is the ability to perform tasks without using your brain's thinking power on the details. It is automaticity that permits you to walk and talk, ride a bike or drive a car and talk in your native tongue at the same time without specifically thinking about the process. Automaticity is an adjunct of muscle memory, and it comes through practice.

The U. S. hockey team acquired automaticity—and won the Olympics—because Herb Brooks made them practice. And practice. And practice some more. The team did so many board-to-board sprints, they called them "Herbies."

Brooks united his team in purpose, gave them the strength, muscle memory and, eventually, the *automaticity* to perform at an almost subliminal level. "Practice beats talent," Brooks preached, "when talent doesn't practice."

How does this apply to you, the student of Mastery? It means you don't have to be a genius to succeed in your mission. You don't require a miracle. But you *do* have to apply vision, desire, compassion, flexibility and . . . *practice*.

But there's more. Practice in itself is not the entire solution. Muscle memory and automaticity are indiscriminate phenomena. They can deliver bad results just as they can good. Practicing wrong moves delivers wrong results, just as surely as practicing the right moves delivers right results.

In his best-selling book *Outliers*, Malcolm Gladwell famously asserted that 10,000 hours of practice was the magic number to become an expert in most disciplines. What Gladwell neglected to say was that unless those hours are spent practicing the correct moves, you only become good at repeating your mistakes.

The old adage "Practice makes perfect" should be amended: "*Perfect* practice makes perfect."

Putting it Together

The combination of mental and physical practice leads to greater performance improvement than does physical practice alone, a phenomenon for which our findings provide a physiological explanation.
—ALVARO PASCUAL-LEONE,
Professor of Neurology at Harvard Medical School

Here comes another hard truth: every worthwhile mission requires application, both physical and mental. There are no pills, shortcuts, or silver bullets. In recent times old-fashioned learning techniques—drills, memorization, rote learning—have gotten a bad rap, conjuring images of teachers with hickory sticks and students with dunce caps singsonging multiplication tables and state capitols.

The images are misleading. Despite wishful thinking, the inescapable fact remains that becoming an expert at any skill— math, athletics, music, science, language—requires drills. And memorization. And, yes, a certain amount of rote learning.

University of Virginia professor of psychology Daniel Willingham says, "You can't be proficient at some academic tasks without having certain knowledge be automatic—'automatic' meaning that you don't have to think about it, you just know what to do with it."[1]

And how do you acquire that certain knowledge? Here are some ways:

— **Slower is faster**.

You've heard this before. When your mission requires repetitive exercise, whether it's weight lifting or language learning or juggling, *slow* is often the key to success.

Music students must develop muscle memory to reach performance readiness. Music teacher David Motto advises students to begin learning a piece by playing *slowly*, at a tempo allowing them to play the piece perfectly the first time. The tempo is gradually increased, maintaining accuracy, until the student can play at performance tempo.[2]

The key to the slower-is-faster method of practicing is placing a correct, single chunk of information into your memory for each small section of your music. According to neuroscientist and musician Daniel Levitin, the human brain creates the strongest memories with repetition. "The strength of a memory," Levitin says, "is related to how many times the original stimulus has been experienced."[3]

This means the stimulus you send to your brain (the correct playing of a section of music) must be received again and again. The signal must be consistent and repetitive.

— **Association**

In its short term memory mode, your brain gathers information quickly—and forgets the same information just as fast. Muscle memory is different. It requires more time to process, yet once muscle memory is stored, it is rarely forgotten.

Associating new skills with physical objects or positions promotes muscle memory. Students in Super Spanish courses are taught to use a "Latin posture." Because people of every culture have a different way of standing when they talk, Spanish students learn to associate the Latin posture with the language. Once the posture is embedded in their muscle memory and associated with Spanish, the learning flows more easily.

— Visualize
Mental practice can be just as effective as physical practice. The ability to close your eyes and picture every single movement is an important tool in directing your muscles to the desired movements. More on visualization coming up.

— Create Habitual Routines
Develop routines that go from visualization to execution in exactly the same sequence every time. Do everything the same. You want the imprinted muscle memory to be identical each time you execute the technique. Again using the example of learning Spanish, students stand in their Latin posture while learning ten important Spanish phrases each day. It is this association—plus the habit—that equates to *memory*.

— Focus on Quality
Because muscle memory is long term, there's a built-in risk. It means that if you repeatedly execute a task *incorrectly*, you may be storing that incorrect movement into muscle memory. In learning and practicing new skills, insure that you're focusing on quality, not locking incorrect movements into muscle memory. It may be difficult, perhaps impossible, to rid yourself of the wrong movements later. Focusing on quality movements applies to a myriad of skills: music, sports, public speaking, flying, juggling.

What the adage "You can't teach an old dog new tricks" *really* means is that the old dog may have a cache of *wrong* tricks already stored in his muscle memory.

— Maximize memory freedom

Have you ever awakened in the middle of the night and realized that a loved one's birthday was yesterday? Have you forgotten to file a tax form, pay a bill, fulfill an obligation that is past due?

Of course. Such lapses are common. The plague of forgetfulness can be blamed, in part, on the increasingly fast-paced world you live in. Stress has a direct impact on memory and cognitive function. A stress-released hormone called cortisol has been proven to adversely affect brain function, especially memory.[4]

How to maximize your available memory? Any form of stress reduction—meditation, prayer, yoga, hot baths—can improve your brain's ability to retain stored information.

Reduce the requirement to remember dates, meetings, appointments. Use the simple and traditional work-arounds. Memory aids—note books, smart phones, Post-It notes, notations in your calendar, index cards—free your memory so you can use it in creative ways.

Success in the quest for Mastery depends on the success of your missions. Make muscle memory and automaticity key ingredients in the accomplishment of those missions.

---

[1] "In educational circles, sometimes the phrase 'drill and kill' is used, meaning that by drilling the student, you will kill his or her motivation to learn," says Daniel Willingham, quoted in a *New York Times* article about education. Willingham thinks this is all wrong. He approves of drilling as a means of measuring what you've learned. "Testing yourself is really good. It actually leads to better learning than studying."

http://www.nytimes.com/2010/09/19/magazine/19fob-medium-heffernan-t.html?_r=0

2 Some students, not surprisingly, resist the slower-is-faster technique because they think they'll never get through all the material they need to play. Teacher David Motto says, "When I speak to groups of music students about music practice tips, how to learn music, and achieving goals, muscle memory is always one of the main parts of the discussion. When your muscles can correctly and automatically play all the notes in your music, your performances are easier and more fun." Learn Faster by Playing Slower: Muscle Memory Techniques that Work. http://www.moltomusic.com/music-practice-tips/slower-is-faster/

3 "Think of a song that resonates deep down in your being," says Daniel Levitin in his book *This is Your Brain on Music*. "Now imagine sitting down with someone who was there when the song was recorded and can tell you how that series of sounds was committed to tape, and who can also explain why that particular combination of rhythms, timbres and pitches has lodged in your memory, making your pulse race and your heart swell every   time   you   hear   it." http://daniellevitin.com/publicpage/books/this-is-your-brain-on-music/

4 The Cortisol Conspiracy. Renowned brain researcher Robert M. Sapolsky has shown that sustained stress can damage the *hippocampus,* the part of our limbic brain which is central to learning and memory.   The culprits are glucocorticoids, a class of steroid hormones secreted from the adrenal glands during stress. They are more commonly know as corticosteroids or cortisol.

During a perceived threat, your adrenal glands immediately release adrenalin. After a couple of minutes, if the threat is severe or still persists, the adrenals then release cortisol. Once in the brain, cortisol remains much longer than adrenalin and continues to affect brain cells.

Chronic over secretion of cortisol adversely affects brain function, especially memory. Human studies show a correlation between high cortisol levels and decreased memory and cognitive functions like concentration and creativity.
http://www.utmb.edu/psychology/adultrehab/stress_and_your_brain.htm

17

Intuition and Bandwidth

The only really valuable thing is intuition.
—ALBERT EINSTEIN

At the core of all your thoughts, emotions, and actions is the communication between the neurons within your brain. This communication, a pattern of synchronized electrical pulses, generates brainwaves that resonate like tiny drumbeats inside your head. The brainwaves range across a spectrum of four main bandwidths, which can be measured by EEG readings.

Each bandwidth is associated with a specific realm of consciousness. A useful analogy is to think of these frequencies—Beta, Alpha, Theta, Delta—as news channels. Each channel is tuned to a range of news—local, regional, global, universal.

— The Local News: Beta (14-40Hz)

Beta waves are the part of your consciousness that takes care of the here and now, the immediate time and space around you. The Beta bandwidth is a vital tool, essential in the process you call logic. Beta delivers the hugely important knowledge about conditions at any given moment.

You use Beta in active conversation. Debaters, teachers, talk show hosts all are in active Beta when they are engaged in their work. But humankind, especially in the Western world, depends so heavily on Beta—the logic mode—that they ignore the signals (we call them intuition) from your other brainwave frequencies.

Imagine owning a car that could operate on gas, or battery, or solar power, or stored kinetic energy, but lacked a processor to select the optimum mode for any specific condition. The car would never attain maximum efficiency. Nor can you function in your own optimum mode when your brain is powered solely by the logic-bound Beta frequency. For heightened situational awareness, you require different bandwidths.

— The Regional News: Alpha (7.5-14Hz)

The Alpha bandwidth taps into an area of intelligence too vast for your prefrontal logical brain to compute on its own. The Alpha bandwidth serves to reduce stress and increase relaxation. Imagine driving down a freeway when your only view is through the front window. Changing lanes would be highly stressful (and dangerous). But if your view were widened to take in information from the side and rear windows and rear view mirrors, your tension would ease because your *regional* knowledge had expanded.

This can be likened to Alpha state. When you complete a task and sit down to rest, you may enter Alpha. When you meditate you enter Alpha. Taking a slow, thoughtful walk in a garden may place you in Alpha.

Alpha waves are also the source of those intuitive, creative flashes that almost never come from logic-based thinking. Most animals operate on this bandwidth. When an earthquake is imminent, dogs are known to howl. Roosters crow. Birds fly away. Humans have this capability as well, yet most are too steeped in Beta-logic thinking that their natural intuition is shut off. Tapping into the Alpha frequency informs you of events immediately beyond your conscious awareness.

— The Global News: Theta (4-7.5Hz)

The Theta frequencies tap into a deeper, vaster level of intelligence, like a powerful computer that can handle far more data than the underpowered processor in your logical mind.

When you find yourself daydreaming, or driving on a freeway and discovering that you can't recall the last several miles, you are probably in Theta. Theta waves are present during deep meditation and light sleep, including your all-important REM sleep.

It is the realm of your subconscious where you experience the most vivid visualizations, inspirations, insights. Theta can occur when you are jogging, taking a shower, brushing your hair. It is the condition in which your mind feels completely disengaged from the task at hand. Theta is the bandwidth at which you may feel connected to virtually everything that is happening in the world.

— The Universal News: Delta (0.5-4Hz)

Delta waves are associated with your deepest sleep (stages 3 and 4) and a state of unconscious awareness. Delta brainwaves have the slowest frequency but are the highest in amplitude. Just before you go to sleep, you are in low Beta. After you've turned off the lights and closed your eyes, your brainwave frequency descends from Beta, to Alpha, to Theta, until you finally fall asleep and enter Delta.

According to quantum science theorists, the Delta state is where your physical boundaries strip away and you connect with your unconscious mind. Many spiritualists, seers, and parapsychologists assert that Delta sleep is associated with perfect intuition, extra sensory perception, and other psychic phenomena.

Research shows that while one brainwave state may dominate in any given condition, the other three states are present at the same time. Knowledge of these four brainwave states makes it possible to use the special characteristics of each. Like the auto that runs on four different sources of energy, you can be mentally productive across a wide range of activities. You can be intensely focused, relaxed, in a highly creative mode, or deep in restful sleep.

The key is to be able to match your brain activity to the occasion. When you need focus and riveted attention— flying an airplane or performing a delicate hand-eye task—you require the here-and-now focus of Beta. But too much Beta in the mix can create anxiety, increase muscle tension, and raise blood pressure. The ideal state is a ratio of the logic-associated Beta frequency with the calming influence of the Alpha frequency to override tension and produce a state of relaxed concentration.

Likewise, when you need the state of deepest meditation or to enter REM sleep, you want to be in Theta. And not until you've entered sleep and connected with your unconscious mind will you encounter Delta, where you encounter the most profound healing effect.

But, you may ask, is it really possible to enter these brain frequency states at will?

The answer is . . . a qualified *yes*—to the extent that you are able to apply the techniques of meditation, visualization, and Super Thinking. Like all powers of mind, accessing the bandwidths of your brain will require conscious effort and practice.

It's a worthwhile effort. Studying and developing this power equips you with yet another valuable tool in the accomplishment of your missions.

Games and Symbols

The problem with connecting to your deeper reserves of knowledge—the area we call intuition—is that intuitive connections don't usually present themselves in English. Or any other spoken language, for that matter. While the logic-producing faculty of your brain frames problems and situations in words and phrases, your deeper, wiser connections with reality are not constrained by such definitions. These connections work in a more symbolic way.

But how, you might ask, do you extract meaning from symbols? How do you make them useful so that you can integrate them into your logical, language-based brain?

One way is via games. When you play you can create rules that are beyond the norm, outside the box of logic. While at play, your information processing and decision making functions can escape the tyranny of reason.

Play is the ultimate educational hook. When you do something that's fun, without risk, you usually do it better. You let your imagination soar. You see eventualities in enjoyable, risk-free ways. You're free from threat.

Conversely, games *without* the non-threatening element of play lack this potential to soar and reveal new eventualities. Think of most professional sports, which are less game than business. Think of high risk warfare, where experimental strategies can be fatal, versus war games in which unorthodox techniques can be tested without penalty.

Because playing is fun and without threat, you can see future opportunity in expanded ways. By eliminating your fear of the unknown, you're more likely to glimpse those *Aha!* moments and out-of-the-box solutions.

Here's a way you can use play to get business ideas by tapping into your deeper brain frequencies.

Pink Elephants and the Brain Storming Game

The brain storming game is a variation on the yellow padding technique. Use meditation to find solutions that you normally couldn't access in lingual form.

The game goes like this:

> **Step 1:** Write by hand for five or ten minutes everything you can about a problem. The problem can relate to business or art or a personal matter. It's best if you do the exercise by hand, not on a keyboard. Let your fingers be an extension of your mind.

> **Step 2:** Take a ten minute meditation. Alternatively, just sit quietly for ten minutes listening to Baroque largo music. Relax and let your mind wander. Be open and innocent with no expectation.

Step 3: At the end of ten minutes write down whatever is on your mind at that moment. Write as much about it as you can. Write fast. If you wish, sketch a picture of whatever you're thinking. Let the ideas flow. Nothing is too farfetched or over the top.

That's the game. Among those thoughts or images you captured may be an out-of-the-box idea. You may discover an idea that had eluded you before. The idea may be in graphic form, a picture rather than words. Let your mind play with the idea. Frame it in the context of your problem, whether it's business, personal, or creative. Solutions sometimes present themselves in unexpected forms.

Mastery co-author Gary Scott learned this game from a Buddhist monk. The first time Scott tried it, he had been attempting to resolve an investment quandary. As an advisor to several investment managers, he had determined—with his *logical* brain—that investments in certain water companies might be a timely opportunity. But *which* companies? Of the choices, each had its pros and cons.

Scott played the brain storming game. At the end of the game he was left with an image of . . . pink elephants.

Pink elephants? Where did that come from? It made no sense. What did pachyderms have to do with investments?

Nothing. Or perhaps more than he yet understood.

Scott's tutor believed that we are all part of an infinite intelligence, a belief shared by thinkers like Thomas Edison [1]and *Think and Grow Rich* author Napoleon Hill. These geniuses attributed their flashes of inspiration to a reserve of intelligence that they believed resided deep within themselves. And they also believed that some of the greatest intuitive leaps of knowledge came not in the medium of language but in the form of symbols.

But *elephants*? Scott knew that in Eastern tradition the symbol of the elephant related to strength, royalty, and a wise woman as a matriarchal head of family. Additionally, the color pink was historically associated with women and femininity as well as being a color of good health and life.

Scott pondered his investment decision. From the brain storming game had come the image of the pink elephant. Did it mean anything? Was it, in fact, a symbol? Did it have a connection to some deeper intuition?

After dwelling on the pink elephant and its connotation of femininity, Scott made an intuitive choice. He opted for a Singapore water company, which, besides its other positive attributes, happened to have been founded and managed by . . . a woman.

The decision was fortuitous. The price of the shares more than doubled in the next four years. It was a far better outcome than any of his other potential choices would have delivered.

Was Scott's decision, in fact, intuitive? Perhaps. Or perhaps it was a happy coincidence. What is true is that an uncommon number of great ideas and decisions throughout history have been spawned by the mysterious faculty we call intuition. Draw your own conclusions.

And in the meantime try this. Listen to a guided meditation designed to help brain storm ideas and stimulate intuition. Listen to the meditation at

http://www.garyascott.com/2013/01/31/27893.html or select a baroque music composition that includes portions played at a largo tempo.

---

[1] A technique used by Thomas Edison to access his intuition was to sit in a chair holding a ball in each hand while he thought about an unsolved problem. As he began to daydream and then doze off, the balls would drop to the floor, waking him up. Edison would immediately jot

down whatever idea or dream that was in his mind, frequently coming up with inventive new solutions to his problems. http://www.sharonmassoth.net/sharons-blog/develop-a-method-for-your-intuition

18

Zoning

On the flow path we are drawn forward by fire; by powerful hedonic instincts; by our deep need for autonomy, mastery, and purpose deeply fulfilled; by dizzyingly feel-good neuro-chemistry ... to make meaning from experience.
—STEVE KOTLER in *The Rise of Superman*: *Decoding the Science of Ultimate Human Performance*

You remember those moments. They were unforgettable episodes in your life when you felt possessed by a sense of effortlessness. When you somehow transcended your normal physical and mental limits. When you *knew* you were performing at a higher level than you ever thought possible.

Perhaps it was an athletic event. For reasons that seemed miraculous you achieved an unexpected personal record. Or it might have been a cognitive episode in school or at work. Your perceptions and acuities and insights sharpened to such a fine edge that previously unsolvable problems became easy for you. Decisions came fast and sharp. Your mind conjured up solutions with profound clarity.

Were these experiences pure happenstance? Random states of mind that visited you by whim of fate? Or were they manifestations of a condition that can be summoned like a reluctant muse?

The answer is ... *all of those*. What you were experiencing was the phenomenon psychologists have only recently begun to identify. "Flow," "peak experience," being "in the Zone"— these are all descriptions of the same state we'll call Zoning. Zoning is an optimal condition in which your mind and body are functioning at a level beyond their normal limits.

Part of the allure—and mystery—of Zoning is that it is elusive. You don't attain it by taking a course. You don't buy it like a supplement from a health food store. You don't attain it through pills, drugs, or tonics. Nor can you summon it at will—at least not without application and intense motivation. Zoning happens not by divine accident, but by cultivation. The Zone is a source of inspiration, the fuel of high achievement, a compressor of learning time.

Despite Gladwell's premise in *Outliers* that mastering any skill—playing a violin, computer programming, brain surgery—takes 10,000 hours of dedicated practice, reaching expert level in any discipline has less to do with the number of hours of practice than it does with *the mindset during the practice.* Pure repetition without focused attention on improvement won't elevate your skill level beyond a level of basic competence. And reaching that state of focused attention is your key to being in the Zone.

In 1954 when Roger Bannister broke what was believed to be an impossible barrier, the four-minute-mile, he was solidly in the Zone. "I felt that the moment of a lifetime had come," Bannister recalled. "There was no pain, only a great unity of movement and aim. The world seemed to stand still, or did not exist. The only reality was the next two hundred yards of track under my feet. The tape meant finality—extinction perhaps."

The pioneering researcher Dr. Mihály Csíkszentmihályi quoted an unnamed composer who did his best work in the Zone. "You are in an ecstatic state to such a point that you feel as though you almost don't exist," said the composer. "I have experienced this time and again. My hand seems devoid of myself, and I have nothing to do with what is happening. I just sit there watching it in a state of awe and wonderment. And the music just flows out of itself."

MASTERY

The Zone is the region inhabited by inventors, artists, creators, extreme athletes, explorers, problem solvers. It's where the *Aha!* moments occur as regularly as the blooming of flowers. The Zone is the place where high achievers like Leonardo da Vinci, Richard Feynman, Thomas Edison, Isaac Newton, Steve Jobs, Ludwig von Beethoven, Frank Lloyd Wright, Albert Einstein, Mahatma Gandhi found their greatest inspiration.

And so can you.

Enter the Zone

Hell, if it was easy, everyone would be doing it.
— HARRY SHEPARD, air show pilot and aerobatic maestro

Entering the zone at will is *not* easy, and everyone is *not* doing it. As with all worthwhile endeavors, learning to tap this powerful source requires application, persistence, focus. You must be willing to experiment. To take control of your mind and body. And—you knew this was coming, right?—your progress will be greatly aided, as in all Mastery pursuits, if you keep a written record of your efforts.

But can you learn to enter the Zone at will? Emphatically, *yes*. The Zone is a state of mind. Zoning is a process you learn just as you learn to meditate, juggle, fly a helicopter, do a flip turn.

You and you alone are in control of your thoughts, words, feelings. You can choose to be indolent, enthusiastic, depressed, excited, angry. And you can choose the state of mind that sets you up for entering the Zone.

Here are steps that will help you access the Zone.

— *Recall past occasions when you knew you were in the Zone.*
   Those moments are fixed in your mind. They left an indelible memory, even if you didn't attribute your heightened ability to what is now called the Zone. In a

195

meditative state, revisit those special instances in your life. Those events of expanded clarity, effortlessness, precision of movement. Try to relive those experiences in your mind. What were the circumstances that led you to that condition? Did a specific technique facilitate entering the Zone?

— *Believe you can enter the Zone.*

Your belief system can be your most powerful tool in accessing the Zone. Having recalled experiencing the Zone, you *know* that it exists and that you can re-experience the state. Just as the placebo effect invokes the healing power of a medical patient's belief system, the power of your own belief system can propel you into that effortless mind-body state called the Zone. It may take the form of a ritual, a mantra, meditation, or a recalled image that induces the flow of the Zone. What's important is that you *believe* that you can enter the Zone.

— *Make the challenge appropriate to your skill.*

You enter the Zone only when your objective is sufficiently challenging. When you strive for excellence in any mission—a sport, a new skill, a creative accomplishment—be sure you set the bar high enough. Giving yourself a too-easy challenge won't invoke the chemistry you require to slip into the Zone. You must be motivated to rise to a challenge, to seek the next level. It is the ignition of this potent neuro-chemistry that propels you into the Zone.

— *Focus all your attention on the challenge.*

Make the execution of the task the focal point of your consciousness. This requires not only attention but discipline. Train yourself to exclude all distractions—email,

196

phone, trivial tasks—from your attention. Become one with the mission. It is this intensity of focus that creates the state of mind that opens your path to the Zone.

— *Stay with the task.*

Entering the Zone does not happen instantly. It only works when the subconscious takes over from the conscious mind. This may take a few minutes or much longer, depending on the intensity of the task. It is the steady, sustained focus of your attention to the task that eventualy produces the chemistry of the Zone.

Once in the Zone, you gain the sense that you have unlimited potential in your grasp. That you are the master of your fate. That neither age nor circumstance will impede your progress toward Mastery. You'll have found the sweet spot for the execution of every mission.

ROBERT GANDT AND GARY A. SCOTT

19

Super Thinking

Your capacity for learning is enhanced when your body—and your mind—reach a state of relaxation. You can achieve this state through a couple of mental exercises.

Joy of Learning Recall

Return to a moment in your life when you experienced a truly gratifying learning moment. The moment can be recent or long ago. Recall that sense of triumph when you solved a difficult puzzle, scored well on a tough exam, made an exciting discovery. Imagine yourself in that situation again. Recall the sensations of the experience, how you felt, what you were thinking, the eagerness that you sensed. Hold onto that feeling. Let it flow through you. Try to store that feeling in a place where you can retrieve it at will.

Breathing to a Beat

Close your eyes and take a very slow, deep breath through your nose. Inhale as much air as you can. Then try to take in a bit more. Now exhale slowly. Feel a deep sense of relaxation as you exhale. Practice taking these deep breaths. Distend your abdomen. As you slowly exhale, pull your abdomen in. Take another deep breath and hold it for a count of three, then exhale very slowly. Continue inhaling in even and continuous breaths.

Now make your breathing rhythmic. Inhale to a count of four, hold to a count of four, exhale to a count of four, pause to a count of four. After four cadences, try slowing down even more to a count of six. After four cadences, try a count of eight. Repeat four cadences.

The breathing exercise will have the effect of slowing down your body/mind rhythms while producing a condition of relaxed alertness—the ideal state for heightened learning.

Super Thinking and the Baroque Masters

Among the first researchers in the field called Super Thinking was Bulgarian educator and psychiatrist Georgi Lozanov, whose pioneering work in the 1960s and '70s was conducted behind the Iron Curtain and remained mostly unknown to western observers.[1] One of Lozanov's breakthrough ideas was the use of music in strengthening memory and accelerating the rate of learning. Lozanov observed that the slow movements of classical Baroque music—a tempo of roughly one beat per second, sixty beats per minute—produced a calming effect and an optimum state for learning. Examples are found in the music of Bach, Vivaldi, Handel, Corelli, Telemann. Largo movements (slow) are around sixty beats per minute. The potent, rhythmic lilt of the 16th to 18th century compositions had the effect on Lozanov's subjects of a sonic massage, beating like a human pulse.

But there was more. Lozanov discovered not only that music therapy enhanced memory and learning, he also found that the calming effect of the music was beneficial in treating patients with cardio and hypertension problems. Among all Lozanov's subjects—students and patients—he observed the same effect: lowered blood pressure, slower pulse rates, lessened muscle tension, reduction of headaches and pain.

That sound patterns can affect consciousness comes as no surprise to students of music history. A famous tale concerns composer Johann Sebastian Bach and the Russian ambassador to the Dresden court, Count Kayserling. Because Kayserling was in poor health, suffering from insomnia and depression, he asked

Bach to compose pieces for him that might be played by the young harpsichordist, Johann Gottlieb Goldberg. Kayserling requested that the music be of such a soft and lively character that he might be cheered up by them in his sleepless nights.

The composer agreed. Legend has it that the count was so pleased by Bach's compositions—the now-famous "Goldberg Variations"—that he rewarded the composer with a goblet containing a hundred gold coins.

You already know that music is a superb memory and learning tool. How often have you heard a song from twenty, thirty, or forty years ago and in an instant you recalled the lyrics, the tune, even the person you were with when you first heard it?

The key to this memory faculty is a tuning fork phenomenon called entrainment. Entrainment is the automatic mechanism within your body that synchs you with external rhythms, pulses, or beats. Whether you're aware of it or not, you entrain to rhythms around you throughout each day.

Here's an easy way to prove it. Count your heart rate while stuck in traffic, around loud machinery, or listening to blaring, high temp rock music. Count it again while you're relaxing in a soft chair or listening to peaceful music in a quiet environment. Your breathing and heart rates *entrain* with the surrounding frequencies. You synchronize with your environment in much the same way a note struck on a single piano then resonates in the same key with surrounding pianos.

So how do you put this phenomenon to work as a learning tool? One simple technique—the one pioneered by Georgi Lozanov—is to begin your learning session by listening to the largo movements of certain Baroque composers. The continuous rhythm of the sixty-beat-per-minute frequency will have the effect of synchronizing your brainwaves and heart rate with the music. Not coincidentally, this places you in an Alpha-Beta state—the optimum condition for learning.

Give it a full ten minutes or more. Close your eyes. Allow yourself to relax. Let the pulsing waves of the Baroque movements flow over you. When you then turn your full attention to your task, whether it's learning a language, solving a problem of logic, creating a passage of literature, you should find that you are more alert, more lucid, more receptive to knowledge.

Pause to congratulate yourself. And reflect. You've added to your Mastery tool kit yet another instrument—Super Thinking—to assist in each of your missions.

Super Thinking to the Rescue

Real estate broker Suzy Kurinsky found that the techniques she encountered in a Super Thinking/Super Spanish course—Baroque music, guided meditation, relaxed concentration—translated to other learning skills. While finishing the Spanish course, she realized she had overlooked a deadline in her continuing education requirement to maintain her real estate broker's license. The cutoff date for completing the course was a month sooner than she expected, and she had completed only three of the forty-five required units. She had only two days to finish the entire course.

Kurinsky's solution: she applied the same Super Thinking techniques she had just learned in the Spanish course. In the two days before the deadline she completed the remaining forty-two units. Her score: between 90.6 percent and 96 percent on all the tests.

---

[1]   Some of Lozanov's work was revealed in a 1970 book, Psychic Discoveries Behind the Iron Curtain, by Sheila Ostrander and Lynn Schroeder. Many of the book's "discoveries," particularly those relating to Russian use of ESP in espionage activities of the Cold War, have

been challenged or found unsupportable. A later and more objective book by the same authors, *Super-Learning 2000* explores Lozanov's work in a modern light.

20

Super Reading

Mastery is about learning. Since a prime source for learning is the written language, it would seem obvious that accelerating your reading speed increases your rate of learning.

Obvious, but not so simple.

Woody Allen once joked that he had taken a speed reading course. After the course he was able to read *War and Peace* in two hours. "It's about Russia," he said.

Speed reading courses get a bad rap because of the assumed inverse relationship between reading rate and comprehension. It's expected that as your eyes consume larger blocks of text, you retain less of what you read. Words and sentences and paragraphs flash past like subliminal messages. Gone before you've made sense of them.

Part of the problem, at least for westerners, is our phonetic writing system. The marks on a page of text represent meaningless sounds. They take on meaning only after we've gone through the mental process of hearing them in our heads as speech. In other writing systems such as Chinese the marks on the page have symbolic meanings. Seeing the mark for "dog," the reader doesn't have to hear "dog" but actually *sees* the dog. By this means, called the ideographic writing system, people who speak different languages can read and understand the same string of text.

In one way, our system is more powerful. In western languages, *any* word can be represented in marks, even if you don't know the meaning. Anything you can say, you can write—and read. But there's a drawback: all those marks must be translated into speech, which requires mental vocalization. Which means s-l-o-o-w. The ideographic system, although containing vastly more marks, is akin to viewing a picture. Reading about trees, you see the forest. The meaning is instantaneous.

You learned to read your native language as a child first by hearing text read to you. Then you were taught to read to yourself, probably aloud. Even later, after you had grown out of the lip-moving stage, you were still sounding out the written words in your head (called subvocalization). Because of this entrenched connection between letters and sounds, your reading pace has barely exceeded the rate at which you speak and hear words. For the average reader of English, that's somewhere around 200-300 words per minute.

But there's another reason your reading rate is stuck in the low three-digits. You *think* that your eyes move in a straight line across a page of text, drop down and sweep across again, line after line. The reality is that your eyes only focus when they're *not* moving. They actually make tiny, imperceptible hops, stopping to dwell on a small parcel of words, then they move to the next. Each stop lasts a quarter to a half second for most people.

To prove this to yourself, slowly read a line of text with one eye closed. Put a fingertip over the eyelid of the closed eye. You'll feel the tiny, sequential movements and stops of the eyeball as it hops across the line.

Without any training, your eyes may be making as many as five or more hops across a line of book-sized text. That means you are seeing the words of this sentence like this:

That means
you are
seeing the
words of
this sentence
like this:

If you were to take in more words in each hop, then you would be seeing something more like this:

That means you are
seeing the words of
this sentence like this:

Concentrating on separate words, one at a time, causes you to lose some of the overall concept of the text. By expanding the span of each hop, you take in clauses, whole phrases, sentences, approximating the Chinese system in which entire phrases have instant meaning. Larger chunks, fewer hops. Taking in larger chunks per hop not only speeds up your reading, it makes the content more intelligible.

So how do you learn to take in larger chunks? How do you minimize the number of hops your eyes make across a line? How do you speed up the sweep of your eyes over a page?

The best way is . . . you know. Make it a mission. Determine a specific goal. Apply a timeframe. And then, of course, keep a record of your progress.

But first you need a starting point.

The Benchmark

To determine your benchmark reading speed, select a book that will remain open when you lay it flat on the table. Determine word count by counting the words in ten typical lines. Divide by ten to determine average word per line and round it off to the nearest whole digit. Next, count the number of text lines on five pages, then divide by five to determine average lines per page. Multiply the average lines per page by the average word per line. *Voila!* You have the average words per page.

You're ready for your benchmark reading.

Use a timer. Read for exactly one minute at your normal rate, reading for comprehension. At the end of one minute, multiply the lines read by your average words per line. If you want to fine-tune the number, do the benchmark reading two or three times.

And, yes, don't forget to record the words per minute (WPM) in your journal. This is the baseline from which you will measure progress.

Read Faster—Retain More

Speed reading is both a cognitive exercise and a motor skill. As with any motor skill, you must unlearn some old habits. And as you incorporate new techniques, you practice them until they become habit. Cultivate these three basic habits to accelerate your rate of reading—and learning.

1. Use a tracker

Practice reading with a tracking device. Any pointing device will do, but the best is a ballpoint pen with the tip retracted. Imagine you are *underlining* the words in the text while your eyes follow the tip of the pen. The tracker keeps your eyes fixated on the place in the line and sets the pace at which you read. *Keep your eyes on the tracker* while you read. As a motor skill exercise, move the tracker across the page at a rate no slower than *one second per line*. Does this seem too fast? No matter. You're not reading for comprehension at this point. Using the tracker at this speed is the equivalent of weight training for the eyes. When the one-second-per-line rate allows you to comprehend most of the content, then it's time to bump the speed up to half a second per line. For purposes of dramatic improvement, use a practice reading rate of three times the rate at which you *want* to eventually read. If your target rate is 1,000 WPM, do your exercise reading at—yes, it's a stretch—3,000 words per minute.

2. Use soft focus

Most of your waking hours your eyes are spent in hard focus (called foveal vision). Your eyes are locked on the current object of your attention—computer screen, television, smart phone, or . . . page of written text. You need hard focus for observing detail—threading a needle or sighting a gun. In hard focus the muscles of your eyes, face, and neck are contracted. However, when you read in hard focus your peripheral vision narrows to a few words at most.

The concept of soft focus—relaxing your eye muscles and expanding your field of vision without focusing on detail—has many applications in Mastery. It is a skill that can heighten your ability in sports, social contacts, problem solving, and, yes . . . *reading*. Shifting to soft focus mode when you practice super reading, you'll find that your eyes take in greater expanses of text in each fixation. Peripheral vision is expanded. Your mind can dwell on the content, not on individual words. Best of all you'll have the exhilarating feeling of floating down the page, line after line, consuming text like a flower soaking up sunshine.

3. Begin and end each line with an indent

Focusing at the beginning and continuing to the end of the line wastes nearly half your peripheral range. With this drill you are going to expand your peripheral vision to include more words per fixation. By beginning a line of text at least two words into the line and finishing *two words* before the end, you will double your reading rate. With practice you'll be able to indent three or more words from each end, increasing your speed even more dramatically. Here's how:

Begin reading at the same one-second-per-line pace—or faster—but start the tip of the tracker *one* word in from the beginning and end one word from the last word in the line. After a few sessions at that pace, move the indent to *two* words from the beginning and end. As you do these drills, concentrate on consistency and speed without worrying about comprehension. Again, this process is akin to weight training for the eyes. Your challenge is to concentrate on the exercise without letting your mind wander. And don't forget to use soft focus—your key to expanded vision. You'll be taking in multiple words simultaneously, registering images and ideas without translating.

Measure Your New WPM

After you've practiced the Super Reading technique for a week, repeat the speed test. Use the same words-per-line calculation as you did when you established your benchmark WPM. Read at the fastest rate you can and still comprehend the material. You may find that you now *prefer* reading with some sort of tracking device, which is fine. Use all your new skills—soft focus, tracking, indenting the end and beginning of lines.

Record the new WPM. Note the difference from the benchmark number you established a week ago. You should observe an increase in your reading rate. But don't be content with small advances. Resume the exercises until the principles of Super Reading have become an ingrained habit. Continue recording your progress.

Somewhere in the process it will happen: one of those breakthrough moments. You'll be reading—and retaining what your read—at a rate far speedier than ever before.

Take a moment to congratulate yourself. You've just added a critical learning tool in your quest for Mastery.

Part Five

The Anti-Retirement

Don't simply retire from something; have something to retire to.
—HARRY EMERSON FOSDICK

Retirement without the love of learning is a living burial.
— SENECA

21

The Power of the Pinnacle Career

Pinnacle: *noun:* the highest or culminating point, as of success, power, fame: *the pinnacle of one's career.*

It happened so suddenly. You were cruising through age fifty, then fifty-five, accelerating into your sixties when—*Zap!*—your world changed. Your career—or the occupation you considered a career—sputtered to a finish. There was a party, congratulations, jokes, maybe even a watch. And then you were swept along with the eighty-some million Boomers marching off the precipice called retirement.

Something didn't feel right. *Retirement?* In private moments you wondered, *Why should I retire?* An old joke with an embedded truth came to mind: if you're not tired in the first place, why re-tire?

Of course, one reason might be that you truly *were* tired. Like millions of your contemporaries you may have been tired of working too hard at an unfulfilling job. Or tired of zero satisfaction in return for your labor. Tired of a dead end, unrewarding so-called career.

The solution to this kind of tiredness isn't retirement. Nor is it the so-called encore career, which is supposed to be a follow up to your former, real career. This is old age thinking. Mastery changes the entire meaning of concepts like "career" and "retirement."

Part of our old age thinking about retirement derives from a political ploy of the late 1800s. In his quest to unify small states into a powerful empire, Chancellor Otto von Bismarck of Germany created the first welfare state. Bismarck decreed that the government would pay a pension to every non-working citizen over the age of sixty-five.

It was a cheap decree on the Chancellor's part. Few people in those days lived beyond sixty-five.

But the idea stuck. More than a century later Bismarck's arbitrary retirement age remains. A large chunk of the world's population continues to gear their lives toward this event, even though the average life expectancy in developed countries has reached nearly eighty.[1] Ultra-longevity is becoming the norm. People over eighty-five represent 12 percent of the over-sixty-five population, and these oldest of the olds are the fastest growing segment of society.[2] If you live in a developed country, your chance of reaching the century mark increases about 5 ½ percent each year. The number of centenarians doubles every thirteen years.

For a huge number of these seniors, the sweet dream of retirement is turning into an empty promise. A life of directionless activity, endless distraction, passive engagement with the world through television, web-surfing, and inane socializing leaves a tasteless residue. Inevitably they resign themselves to the slow, almost imperceptible erosion of their power and self esteem.

Such a retirement is not only wasteful, it's dangerous. Statistics tell us that people who retire early, especially men, die early. A study of thousands of employees at Shell Oil Company concluded that those who took retirement at age fifty-five *doubled* their risk for death before reaching age sixty-five compared with those who continued working beyond sixty. Another report by the Institute of Economic Affairs (IEA) showed that following an initial boost in health, retirement increases your risk of clinical depression by 40 percent while raising your chances of being diagnosed with a physical condition by 60 percent.[3]

You've reached a special era in history. You live in a time when the value of your life's experience at retirement age is greater than the cost of obtaining it. A few generations ago, people your age were worn out by the process of earning a living.

No more. Because of advanced technology, modern medicine, and your knowledge of how to live a healthy lifestyle, you have a golden opportunity. You can remain active and mission-ready for decades beyond your so-called retirement age.

It's called the Pinnacle Career. It can make you happier, healthier, and longer-lived. Your life will not only be more fulfilled, you may be more comfortable and secure from a continuing income stream.

Never mind retirement. Still ahead is the Pinnacle Career. It's the main event, and you're the star.

Profiles in Mastery

Kathy Royer

Retirement?

For Kathy Royer—pilot, musician, athlete, world traveler—it was an absurd concept. When she hit the mandatory airline retirement age of sixty-five she threw a party. Then she took two days off.

Then she began her next career.

Royer has always been mission-oriented. Her first mission, at age six, was to learn the piano. At ten it was the pipe organ. While earning a degree in music education, it was her mission to become a teacher. While teaching full time and also working as a church organist and choir director, she squeezed in a master's degree in counseling.

But something was still missing. Royer lacked a mission that was truly fulfilling.

And then one day, on a whim, she took a flying lesson. From then on Royer had an ongoing mission in her life. And it came with a price, she learned. Flying lessons were expensive, so she had to work several jobs—teaching, waiting tables, playing the organ in church. Her social and personal life suffered. Her marriage dissolved.

Royer persevered. She quit teaching to be a full time flight instructor. She found jobs as a charter pilot, corporate pilot, and eventually pilot for the governor of Pennsylvania with the title of Director of Training. All the while she continued adding credentials, including commercial and instructor's ratings in helicopters.

In 1987 Royer made the jump to the airlines. She became Pan Am's first female cockpit crewmember on the Boeing 747. After the airline's demise in 1991, Royer started afresh at United Airlines, working her way up from the bottom of the copilot list to the captain's seat. By her retirement she was an FAA-designated line check airman.

Credit: R.Gandt

Royer's first anti-retirement mission was to become certified as a corporate jet flight instructor and examiner. Meanwhile she added to her list of earthbound missions— trekking across New Zealand, over the Andes, down the Grand Canyon; long distance bike races in Florida; triathlon competitions in which she regularly wins medals in her age class.

Royer's list continues. In her recently acquired sport airplane she has learned formation flying and aerobatics. Other new missions include learning German, ballroom dancing, advanced computer skills, and becoming an accomplished public speaker.

Isn't that enough? "Life is short," Royer says. "I don't plan to waste any of it. I'm going to keep learning, stay active, make the most of what I have."

Go for the What?

Chase the vision, not the money; the money will end up following you.
　　　　—TONY HSIEH, co-founder, Zappos.

You heard it at an early age. *Go for the money.* The idea was that success in any career was defined by tiers of wealth. Go for the money and good things would follow—cars, houses, cruises, jewelry, prestige, and privilege. Best of all, you would feel fulfilled, right?

By now you've learned the truth. *Go for the money* was a fraudulent siren song, but it's still the driver behind many freshly launched careers.

Mastery presents you with a different and vastly more powerful driver. By applying your energy to a worthwhile mission, you'll be investing the best of yourself into the activity. A mission-driven career will define value and deliver profits that far exceed pure monetary gain. Ironically, by *not* chasing the money and by directing your talent and energy to your mission, the possibility of *real* monetary profit will be more likely.

That's why a Pinnacle Career—powered by your passion and belief in your own worth—can be your optimum experience. Instead of making money your first and foremost objective, you're making the *mission* your priority.

The success of your Pinnacle Career rests on three bedrock principles.

Principle #1: Put the mission first.

> *Be a missionary, not a mercenary.*
> JOHN DOERR, Venture Capitalist

Jeff Bezos, founder of Amazon.com, is a believer in the power of missions. In 1994 thirty-year-old Bezos left a lucrative job with a hedge fund in Manhattan and moved to Seattle where he started Amazon.com in a garage. He had three simple objectives: Beat the tax man (hence the move to Washington State). Tap into the exploding growth of the internet. Fulfill a mission.

Success didn't come automatically. Amazon's profits soared, plunged, took off again, sputtered again. Bezos went billions in the hole. He stuck to his mission. Amazon grew to become the dominant force in the world of e-commerce. Today Bezos is listed as one of the wealthiest people in the world.

To Bezos, it's all about missions. "I strongly believe that missionaries make better products," he says. "They care more. For a missionary, it's not just about the business. There has to be a business, and the business has to make sense, but that's not why you do it. You do it because you have something meaningful that motivates you."

Bezos's key to success in business? "Care, invest in, and work at something that is meaningful to you."

Principle #2: Make sure the mission is *your* mission.

Missions are the spark plugs of a productive life. You must be certain, however, that they fulfill *your* purpose and not some purpose that others have chosen for you. Missions that bring fulfillment, health, and, yes, wealth succeed if they truly are your mission.

Thus the second principle in building your Pinnacle Career: determine *your* purpose—for earning, learning, living. Don't allow yourself to be distracted from your purpose by the chorus of naysayers that inevitably attend every new enterprise.

Look for your unique path. Look for subtle clues and coincidences. Pay attention to intuition. Stay in touch with how you feel as much as how you think. Mastery is about escaping the tyranny of reason.

Do your friends, family, colleagues think your mission is too . . . *bizarre*? Smile. Consider the words of the Sufi poet, Rumi: "Start a large, foolish project, like Noah. It makes absolutely no difference what people think of you."

Principle #3: Start your own mission-driven business.

Too young to retire, too old to start over. If you're over fifty, you probably know this scenario. It's the Boomers' dilemma. Comfortable jobs with comfortable salaries become increasingly scarce. Skills and qualifications acquired over a lifetime become passé. Your applications are passed over in favor of younger employees who will do the job for less money. Looking for a job becomes a fruitless and demoralizing experience.

The solution? Stop looking. Become your own employer and hire yourself. Start your own business.

The biggest requirement is a change in your mindset. Because you are the boss, you must determine the course of your business. Your mission serves as your compass. Like Jeff Bezos, you are the captain, the navigator, and perhaps in the beginning, the crew of your flagship startup business. Starting your own mission-driven business is the very essence of Mastery in action.

Whoa, you say. Not so fast. *Start a business at my age? I'm not a kid like Bezos when he started Amazon.*

There has never been an age limit on entrepreneurship. The principles of Mastery apply to founding a business just as they do to any mission-driven activity. Your age is not only *not* a handicap in starting a mission-driven business, your experience and acquired skills over the year provide you with a built-in advantage.

But what if I don't have access to large amounts of investment capital?

Given today's technology and digital tools, you can start a micro business on a shoestring budget—and grow it like a carefully nurtured new plant. We'll discuss some of the aspects of a micro business in the next chapter. For now, understand that investment capital is not your most urgent concern in founding a successful micro business.

How do I know whether I'll be successful? Or become rich?

Short answer: you don't. And that's part of the adventure. By applying the principles of Mastery, using your passion and talent as the drivers of your small business, you will exponentially increase your chances of success. Small business owners, according to the late Dr. Thomas J. Stanley, author of *The Millionaire Mind*,[4] have among the *highest* probabilities of gaining real wealth.

During his research Stanley interviewed 733 millionaires to identify the reasons behind their success. Of the millionaires interviewed, corporate executives comprised only 16 percent. Lawyers amounted to another 9 percent, physicians 8 percent. A startling 32 percent of Stanley's millionaires—more than twice as many as in any other category—were small business owners.

Okay, you say, but you have doubts. And more questions. *Maybe a micro business really is the key to a Pinnacle Career, but what kind of business? Where do I begin?*

Again, it's simple. Begin with what you love. You'll see how in the next chapter.

---

[1]   Is U.S. longevity *really* lower than in most other countries? The adage about the three types of prevarications—lies, damned lies and statistics—kicks in here. In studies comparing US longevity with sixteen peer countries including Australia, Austria, Canada, Denmark, Finland, France Germany, Italy and Japan, the average US Longevity is lowest.

This statistic, however, omits part of the story. Most of the lifespan shortfall stems from early deaths before age fifty. Of the subject countries, U. S. infant mortality is highest. Fewer US children reach age fifty because of violence and injuries. Teen pregnancies and SID were also higher than the other countries. Diabetes was higher among adults aged twenty and older. And because American children can begin driving at age fourteen whereas in most countries the earliest age is eighteen, Americans are four times as likely to die in an accident. Americans are also twenty times as likely to die by a gun shot.

But after age seventy-five, the story changes. Beyond age seventy-five, the United States *leads* most other countries in longevity. 2013 CIA Factbook.

[2]   If you made it to your 65th birthday, you can expect to be around for your 81st birthday if you are male, and for your 84th if you are female. The older you are, the longer you are likely to live. Make it to age 75 and you can expect to make it past 85. Make it to 85 and you are

likely to be alive in your 90s. http://www.nia.nih.gov/research/publication/global-health-and-aging/living-longer

3   According to Harvard Professor of Public Policy Lisa Berkman, social isolation is a significant factor in longevity. If you're socially isolated, you're likely to have poorer health and a shortened lifespan. Staying socially connected with those around you keeps you happy and also keeps your brain active and challenged. One example was Walter Breuning, who lived to be 114, who believed that keeping his mind and body busy was one of the key secrets to staying healthy. But for many, retirement means a sudden loss of many work-related social ties and a drastic *decrease* in activity levels. http://articles.mercola.com/sites/articles/archive/2013/05/30/retirement.aspx - !

4   Thomas J. Stanley, who died in 2015, taught marketing at the University of Tennessee, University of Georgia and Georgia State University before pursuing his research of America's wealthy population. *The Millionaire Next Door* by Stanley and William Danko made the *New York Times's* Best Sellers list. http://www.amazon.com/Millionaire-Next-Thomas-Stanley-Ph-D-ebook/dp/B00CLT31D6/ref=sr_1_1?s=books&ie=UTF8&qid=1410105359&sr=1-1&keywords=millionaire+next+door

22

Following Your Passion.

Definition of entrepreneur: someone who will work twenty-four hours a day for themselves to avoid working one hour a day for someone else.
— CHRIS GUILLEBEAU in *The Happiness of Pursuit*

What do you love to do? What is that over-the-top fantasy that still smolders inside you like an ancient spirit? Where is that grandly ambitious idea you had about founding a business that would continue to grow after you're gone? What activity—sport, work, hobby, relationship—most fills you with joy?

It's time to dust off those old fantasies. Examine them in a fresh light. Test each one. Do you see in any of them the kernel of a new enterprise? The making of a mission? If so, embrace it, roll it around in your daydreams, savor the images that flow from it. Retreat to your yellow pad and jot whatever ideas come to mind. Let the ideas flow.

Does it ignite your passion? Is it something you love? Does it hold the key to a micro e-business? A Pinnacle Career?

If you love golf, for example, you could write and publish something related to the game. Do you love travel? Fishing? Dogs, dolls, art? Write and sell specialized publications in these fields. Do you have a passion about social issues—poverty, war, crime, the environment? Start a blog addressing these concerns. Would you like the world to be a more spiritual place? Publish a journal, write a book (or commission one), record a video. Promote your message in a way that enlightens your audience.

Follow your passion.

Your Pinnacle Career can turn your passion into profit by allowing you to do what you really want to do. If your passion, let's say, is for the sport of fishing, you might follow in the footsteps of these micro business entrepreneurs.

John and Mary Lou Blackwell, fishing enthusiasts and outdoor adventurers, grew up in the Oregon mountains. Looking for a way to match their passion to profit, they moved to Canada where they homesteaded 1,200 acres on a trout-filled lake in mid-British Columbia. The Blackwells built and manage a successful fishing camp that attracts sports fisherman from around the world.[1]

Jim Slater, who loved salmon fishing, found a way to turn his passion into a business. Slater bought fishing beats on the River Tay, a legendary Scottish salmon river, offering time shares for fisherman from Britain, Europe and the US.[2] Slater continued to add additional fishing time shares to his portfolio, turning his passion into a hugely profitable enterprise.

Ralph Kylloe, an aficionado of fishing and photography, melded his two passions into a lucrative business. *Fishing Camps*, published by Gibbs Smith, is one of over a dozen lavishly illustrated books produced by Kylloe. Kylloe's micro business allows him to travel around the country indulging his love for fishing as he photographs and writes about it.[3]

Steve Ambrose, yet another fishing entrepreneur, loved to travel. Constrained by family commitments at home, Ambrose set up a bass fishing business in Florida that served Americans, Germans, Canadian, Dutch and Belgians. Later as his children grew and left the nest, Ambrose used his built-in client base to organize and market fishing trips to Argentina .

Each of these entrepreneurs came from different backgrounds. Each varied in age, situation and skills. Their common link was the love of a sport. They managed to blend their unique natures and skill sets into a business that provided them with fun, like-minded clientele—and profit.

Funky Business

Making money in your underwear is a very empowering thing.
—RICHARD SULLIVAN, *Geezercize*

Mission-driven businesses are born from ideas. Sometimes it's those off-the-wall, over-the-top ideas that distinguish successful businesses from failures. Let your Pinnacle Career be as different from the norm as you choose. Your mission can be unpredictable and surprising. Even funky.

How funky? Take Marty and Kris Travis. Their mission was to save the Illinois farm that had been in their family for 179 years before it was sold by a grandparent to a developer. While reacquiring and restoring the farm, the Travises were asked to help eradicate an invasive weed called wild ramp. In the process, they discovered a *demand* for the plant. They wound up selling more than 4,000 pounds of ramps to Chicago restaurants.

Thus was born yet another mission. Following their interest in exotic edibles, the Travises expanded their farming business to include crops like Kickapoo beans and white Iroquois corn. Acting on their passion for unusual farm-grown produce, the Travises not only ignited a thriving new business, they became founders of movement called Stewards of the Land, a group of farm families who market their produce through the Travis family business.[4]

Okay, you may be thinking, it's easy to start a farming business if you already own a farm. Then consider this example of a business founded on little more than a web site—and bubble soap. Sterling Johnson had discovered the wonders of bubbles in a high school science project. Calling himself the "Bubblesmith," Johnson developed a money-making business blowing bubbles at variety shows, corporate events, and private parties. Ultimately Johnson's business took him all over the world, including a high-visibility performance in Washington DC for a congressional picnic.

Another off-the-wall idea was dreamed up by artist Kit Williams. For a book he called *Masquerade*, Williams created a beautiful, golden bejeweled hare, buried somewhere in England in 1980. He filled the book with fifteen examples of his own artwork, each containing a clue to the whereabouts of the golden hare. The book was a huge success, launching a worldwide treasure hunt for the buried hare and eventually triggering a law in the U. K. to head off the hordes of book-reading treasure hunters who were digging up public forests and private gardens.[5]

The Golden Rule of Simplicity

So you've identified the object of your passion. It's something *you* desire to do. With that desire comes a problem: how do you fulfill that desire?

You fulfill it by following the Golden Rule of Simplicity: *Let your desire lead you to the creation and sale of your product.*

Let's say that your passion—and desire—is fishing in exotic locations. Your problem? Satisfying that desire, which means finding, affording, and transporting yourself to those exotic locales. Somewhere within that problem—and its solution—you will find the seed of your new product or service.

Using the fishing example, your solutions might include. . .

— *Being a fishing guide, taking customers to the prime locales.*

— *Being a publisher of maps and guide books pointing readers to the best places.*

— *Being a packager and deal-maker, marketing tours for existing fishing services.*

— *Creating your own chain of fishing camps.*

Your imagination—and desire—will come up with dozens of solutions. And your problem—satisfying your passion for fishing—will identify your potential customers.

How? Because they're people just like you. Because they have the same problem—and desire—as you. You already have a wealth of knowledge about them.

Okay, having identified these customers, how do you find them? Easy. They are like-minded souls with whom you share a common passion. They visit the same sites, publications, gathering spots as you. They will be the foundation of your new customer base.

But first you have to get their attention. And how, you ask, do you do that?

The old-fashioned way. You tell a story.

---

1   Moose Lake lodge, 300 miles north of Vancouver, British Columbia, is rustic and spacious, and overlooks Moose Lake, filled with one-pound rainbow trout and surrounded by a habitat famous for bald eagles. The lodge offers superb fishing and is a center for fly-outs to fish nearby streams for rainbow trout, cutthroat, steelhead, and salmon. http://www.mooselakelodge.com/your.html

2   Jim Slater became a multimillionaire when he built his investment firm, Slater Walker Securities, into one of the fifty largest companies in the UK. When his business suffered fatal losses in the real estate market in the early seventies, Slater became a minus-millionaire, owing a million pounds more than his assets were worth.

Slater repaid all of these debts with interest within a couple of years. He formed a joint venture that grew to own and manage over 1,500 apartments in London. His love of salmon fishing led him to turn the property management skills gained in the apartment business towards management of fishing timeshares on Scottish rivers. http://www.jimslater.org.uk/articles/timeshare-fishing-trout-salmon-june-2009/

3   Ralph Kylloe is the author of fourteen previous books, including *Adirondack Home, Hickory Furniture, Cabins and Camps, Rustic Artistry for the Home, The Rustic Cabin, Rustic Traditions, Rustic Furniture Makers*, and *Fly Fishing the Great Western Rivers*. He is also a foremost authority on rustic furniture and owner of the Ralph Kylloe Gallery at Lake George, in New York's Adirondack Mountains. http://www.ralphkylloe.com/books/books.html

4   Our original purpose can evolve into a great surprise. When the Travis family bought back their families 179-year-old farmstead from developers, their only intention was to renovate the dilapidated farm buildings. The restoration process created a farming community as well. *New York Times Field Report: Family Heirlooms*

5   Kit Williams's book, long out of print, is still a sought-after children's' classic. http://www.amazon.com/MASQUERADE-Kit-Williams/dp/080523747X/ref=sr_1_1?s=books&ie=UTF8&qid=1413831842&sr=1-1&keywords=masquerade

23

What's *Your* Story?

Stories. They've been with us since the dawn of civilization. Your ancestors told them around campfires. They drew them on walls. They carved them in stone. Stories were how they made sense of the world around them. Stories were how they acted out their passions.

And stories are the key to marketing your product. Your passion, whether it's bullfighting or cooking or hot air ballooning, has a story to go with it. The product or service or brand that grows from that passion needs a story to promote it.

But not just any story. A good story gives your business a big voice. Good storytelling and good marketing are intertwined.

To be effective, your story must :

Be short

> You live in the information era, which has produced the internet, smartphones, and social media. And after only about thirty years, this era is reaching maturity. The competition for consumers' attention has reached a melting point. Every product and brand has its own story. Consumers are inundated with stories. To get—and keep—the attention of your potential customers, make your story short and powerful.

Create credibility

> Your story must be authentic. It must be *real.* A good story brings data to life and makes it believable for the skeptical customer.

Be up to date

Like all eras, the information era continues to evolve. Products, technologies, media change constantly. Stories and the products they promote become passé overnight. Make sure your story stays up to date with the rapidly changing age in which you live.

Sell the perception, not the product.

Consumers often buy products based more on story than on technical merits. They are drawn to stories that appeal to their self image. Watch buyers seldom shop for the cheapest or most efficient timepiece. They want a watch that reflects their self image. Those who see themselves as rugged individualists may favor a shock proof watch, water resistant to 300 feet, never mind that the wearer will never venture deeper than the shallow end of the pool. Those who perceive themselves as world-exploring adventurers might choose a massive chronograph with enough dials and navigational aids to take them to Mars. Car aficionados care more about a car's story, how it reflects their self image, than they do about practicality. The best stories aim at perception, not product.

Define the brand

Your story is a signpost for your brand. In the 1950s, R. J. Reynolds ruled the tobacco business with their top-selling cigarette brand, Winston. The Phillip Morris company was an obscure British tobacco firm with a fractional share of the American market. Their Marlboro brand was targeted for women smokers with the slogan "Mild as May." Under new management, Phillip Morris rewrote the Marlboro story. The ladylike image was replaced with the iconic Marlboro Man. A whole new community of smokers embraced the Marlboro aura of manliness, independence, ruggedness. Propelled by its new story, Marlboro became the best-selling tobacco brand in the world.

Build a Community

Communities form around consumers' personal values. Businesses have learned that customers make buying decisions for ethical or cultural reasons as much as for economic value. Corporations who foster causes—environmental awareness, anti-obesity, animal rights—attract customers who share those values. An example is Ben & Jerry's Ice Cream, whose promotion of GMO labeling, marriage equality, and climate justice has attracted a community of loyal activists.

Perception and story—these are the two links that create and bind your community. When it was revealed that famed French Perrier mineral water contained pollution from the process of adding carbonation, the community of Perrier-lovers felt betrayed. Their perception of the mineral water's legendary spring-fed bubbliness had been based on a bogus story, and they took out their rage on Perrier.

Be sure the story of your product reflects a value that your customer can embrace. And be sure the story is true.

Find a Niche

You live in an era of savage competition. A prime example is the cutthroat market for consumer electronics. Think Kindle, Nook, Sony, Samsung, Google, Apple, and more. Their marketplace is a battleground, and each manufacturer has its community of soldiers.

Which means that the startup marketer shouldn't go head to head with the Goliaths on their battlefield. Instead, look for mini-markets the megacorps have overlooked or ignored. Find a niche you can exploit. Then assemble your own community of loyal soldiers around it.

Consider this entrepreneur who took on the medical establishment—but in one of its smallest niches. April Wier's passion was to draw attention to a little known genetic defect called MTHFR— an acronym for an unpronounceable condition called MethylTetraHydroFolate Reductase Polymorphism. Wier's story: "When I was diagnosed with MTHFR gene mutation, I learned very quickly that most doctors don't know very much about it. If you have MTHFR Deficiency, you will enjoy a much fuller life if you become an expert on your body.[1]

The product? Wier's own book about the MTHFR disorder. Her book—and the story that pointed consumers to it—galvanized a small but intensely loyal community of supporters.

Or take Steve Barwick, who sold natural health products via his website. Analytics showed that Barwick's site was drawing only a minuscule number of visitors. Worse, 72 percent of them were leaving the site in the first couple minutes.

And then he found a niche. Barwick zeroed in on a little-known health issue and gave it a story: *A Powerful Healing Discovery that Will Change Your Life— and Your Health— for the Better ... Forever.* In his story, Barwick shared a passionate personal account about how his product helped his wife.

The effect was dramatic. Nearly twice as many viewers who landed on his site were sticking around reading Barwick's story— and learning more about his product. Sales from the web site soared to five times what they'd been.

The Evolutionary Circle of business

Here's the path by which ideas—fueled by passion—evolve into business reality.

— **Ideas lead to enthusiasm . . .**

— **Enthusiasm leads to education . . .**

— **Education leads to action . . .**

— **Action leads to profit or loss—and experience . . .**

— **Experience leads full circle to *more* ideas.**

Profiles in Mastery

Lessons from Felix

photo: Danny Bird for The Heart of England Forest

Go try things.

That was the message—and lifestyle—of British entrepreneur Felix Dennis. When Dennis passed away in 2014, he left an estate of more than $800 million, including a sixteenth-century thatched manor near Stratford-upon-Avon, a London house, a Manhattan apartment, houses in Connecticut and a house on the Caribbean island of Mustique. Dennis's company was publishing more than fifty magazines with revenues over $100 million.

The first lesson to be drawn from his career is that humble beginnings need not be a problem. Abandoned by his father, Felix Dennis grew up in his grandparent's home without electricity or indoor plumbing. His formal education ended at age fifteen. The teenager subsisted on work as a gravedigger, sign painter, and a blues drummer until landing his first real job—selling copies of Oz magazine on the street. A hard worker, young Dennis rose to the position of advertising manager within a year. Before he'd turned twenty-one he had become an editor at the magazine.

And then came calamity—and the second lesson from Dennis. You can make mistakes in your career—and still succeed. Dennis's calamity happened when, for one issue of Oz, the editors allowed teenager readers to choose the content. One of their choices was a cartoon showing a bear's genitalia. Dennis wound up being tossed in jail and convicted of corrupting public morals.

The scandal might have been the end of Dennis's publishing career. Instead, it resulted in a howl of public indignation over the censure of the magazine and the moral charges against the editor. Celebrities including John Lennon and Yoko Ono organized loud street protests. An appeals court eventually tossed out Dennis's conviction, and the wave of publicity turned the young editor into a counter culture hero.

The third and most important lesson to be learned from Dennis's career is go try things. He tried publishing underground comics—and failed miserably. He kept trying. After noticing how teenagers lined up in the early morning to see movies with the legendary martial arts performer, Bruce Lee, Dennis flew to Hong Kong to meet the legendary martial art actor. Within a few weeks he had acquired enough material to start a magazine he called the Kung-Fu Monthly. The magazine was a runaway success. It sold millions of copies in over a dozen countries and laid the foundation for what would become Dennis's publishing empire.

---

[1] April Wier is a writer, blogger, entrepreneur, and student of alternative medicines.

http://aprilwier.hubpages.com/hub/top-10-books-for-mthfr-mutants

24

Staying Mission Capable

Successful entrepreneurs stay in the game by pursuing achievable missions and living within their means. This means their business goals are realistic, and they keep their fledgling businesses afloat by maintaining control of overheads. By growing at a controlled pace, the startup entrepreneur has the time and opportunity to gain mastery over his mission.

Wait a minute, you say. *Aren't we talking about passion and imagination? What's wrong with shooting for the moon?*

Nothing—if you can make it all the way to the moon. The truth is, the majority of startup businesses fail not because of a lack of passion or imagination. They crash and burn because the founder failed to protect the company's assets during its precarious early growth. Enthusiasm, hubris, and lack of mission control permit spending to outrun assets. Like an under-fueled rocket, the company sputters and falls back to earth.

A startup business—especially a Pinnacle Career business—is best begun on a small scale, then carefully nurtured like a sapling while it gains size. The riskiest time for a new company isn't during the initial launch, but after it's taken off. Too often the post-launch phase becomes a time of extravagant spending, of unrealistic expansion, of self indulgence. Overhead and debt bring the fledgling company down.

Here are ways to keep your mission-driven business running within its means:

— **Look for every way you can to trim expenses.**
   Ignore the siren song of unnecessary spending. As your business gains traction, you will be bombarded from every side to spend, spend, spend. Resist with all your might.

Don't let your precious startup enterprise flounder in a sea of bills and debt.

— **Be neither inflexible nor proud.**

During the dot-com bubble, Fred S., a trader who started with zero net worth, built a business worth $300 million. When the bubble burst in the early 2000s, Fred's fortune vaporized. Though he was back where he started, Fred had gained a vast amount of experience. His next mission should have been even more successful, right? Wrong. Fred had become money driven instead of mission driven. When he still had a fortune, at least on paper, Fred had also acquired dangerously bad financial habits. Despite losing his company, he clung to the old habits. Those habits eventually sabotaged his next attempt to found a successful business.

— **Always save.**

Benjamin Franklin had it right. No matter how tough or prosperous the times, strive to save at least 10 percent of your income. It's a simple rule. Stick to it and you will survive almost all deadly economic perils.

— **Look harder for the silver lining.**

The truth about economic cycles? There are more opportunities in bad times than in good. Yet, one of the costliest effects of a recession or a business downturn is the can't-win attitude inflicted on the startup entrepreneur. An old British saying goes, "Where there is muck there is brass." In business, this means that opportunity is found by identifying problems. Difficult economic times create plenty of problems, all begging for solutions. Make it your mission to find those problems—and their solutions.

— **Remain true to your mission**.

When economics shift, when the inevitable business cycles take you on a roller coaster ride, adhere to the principles of Mastery. Stick to your mission plan. As with every mission, continually review your progress, make fine adjustments, and keep your sights on the objective.

You live in the richest, most incredible era mankind has ever known. The world's poorest have more than the richest of a few centuries ago. It's easy to forget your mission when you're caught in a day-to-day struggle to stay afloat. The premise of a Pinnacle Career is doing what you love and learning to earn money from it. When times are tough and the economy slumps, allow yourself to tilt back, at least for a few moments, and ask: *What do I really want to do with the rest of my life?* The answer may be: *This. I'm doing exactly what I want to do.*

Spurts

Most businesses don't gain success in a single spectacular surge of growth. More often, young companies experience an undulating growth pattern—progress followed by setback followed by more progress.

Success comes in spurts, and spurts can be the most dangerous times for startups. Sudden spurts in income can throw your mission off track. You may mistakenly believe that the influx of cash is a one time windfall and, out of fear, halt your company's growth. Your emphasis becomes to *avoid mistakes* rather than continuing to apply Mastery to your enterprise.

But there's a worse mistake. As the cash rolls in you may be tempted to believe you're connected to a never-ending money faucet. Out of hubris you hire new staff. You move to elegant new quarters. You indulge yourself with cars, homes, an unrealistic lifestyle. Money replaces mission.

Inevitably comes the reversal. *Zzztt!*—the lights of the once prosperous company go dark.

Here's a simple formula for creating financial discipline. When you experience a spurt in cash inflow, immediately spend 10 percent of the new money on something *outside* your mission. Buy the Porsche, take the cruise, build the new house. Splurge. Do whatever appeals to you—*as long as it amounts to no more than 10 percent of your new wealth.*

Second, give another 10 percent to a charity or foundation that represents your own values. Since your Pinnacle Career has turned your passion into profit, the donation will have the effect of increasing that passion.

Third, invest the remaining 80 percent conservatively. Or use it to pay off debt. The investment will be your capital for your next and better mission.

Do this and you'll not only be following Ben Franklin's sage advice, you'll be on a sure path to success in your Pinnacle Career.

25

The Writing Mission

There are three difficulties in authorship: to write anything worth publishing – to find honest men to publish it – and to get sensible men to read it.
—CHARLES CALEB COTTON

Writing is an integral component of Mastery. For every proposed mission you write a mission plan. For each activity you write a journal of your progress. For every unsolvable problem, you write ideas until you find a solution. Writing is thinking, and it's an essential tool in keeping you focused and committed to your mission.

Can writing also *be* a mission?

Think back again to that secret trove of dreams you kept hidden away. Was being a teller of stories one of those dreams? Was becoming a writer a fantasy that you entertained, then abandoned? Perhaps you even gave it a shot, maybe wrote part of a novel or a memoir or a history.

And then what happened?

Inertia. The actual process of writing, of spending thousands of hours alone with your ideas, of laboring to produce a publishable work ... it all seemed too daunting. Too incompatible with the realities of making a living and raising a family. You put writing aside, telling yourself you'd take it up again someday. Someday when you had time. Someday when inspiration struck.

That someday never came. Life moved on.

Is it too late? Could you dust off that secret dream, give it another shot? At this point in your reading of Mastery, you know the answer. It's not only *not* too late, there may never be a better time to realize your unfulfilled ambitions. And the best way to convert a nearly forgotten ambition to reality is to make it a mission.

Is writing a suitable mission for you? Let's find out.

The Yin and Yang of Writing

The unread story is not a story; it is little black marks on wood pulp. The reader, reading it, makes it live: a live thing, a story.
—URSULA K. LE GUIN

Modern writing embraces two separate disciplines—the *craft* of writing and the *business* of writing. Just as the artist draws on the right hemisphere of the brain and the businessman uses the left, so it is with the modern writer. Your creative side, the part of you that concocts stories and converts ideas to written words, must work in concert with your business side, the part that markets your product to readers.

The activity we call "writing" is actually a boundless activity that ranges from ancient hieroglyphics to jottings on jailhouse walls to heart-rending romance novels. Before you take up the craft, you must first zero in on your genre. Are you interested in writing a memoir? A family history? A novel based on your experience or on something you know? A how-to book about a field in which you have expertise? Establish your genre.

Next, identify your audience. Aspiring writers can be heard saying things such as, "I don't care whether anybody ever reads what I write. I write for myself." Which might be laudable—if their objective was to have one-way conversations with themselves.

Commercial writing is a pact between two parties—author and reader. "I can't write without a reader," declared novelist John Cheever. "It's precisely like a kiss—you can't do it alone."

Having identified your audience, you have a mental target for your work. Your book's voice, level of technical detail, degree of emotion will be different in a military adventure novel than in a Harlequin romance, just as the readers of each genre are different. Know your readers, and you'll know how to tell them a story. Every modern writer is a descendant of stone age storytellers who mesmerized their fellow cavemen with campfire tales of mastodons and sabre-tooth tigers.

But wherefrom comes that skill to mesmerize your audience? Are some writers naturally gifted wordsmiths? Are some people, like the stone age narrator, natural storytellers? Is there an age limit to becoming a successful writer?

No to all of the above. Writing is a skill that must be learned, and it can be learned at any age. Here's how.

Writing: the Craft

Start writing, no matter what. The water does not flow until the faucet is turned on.
— LOUIS L'AMOUR

Writing publishable content is not an innate talent. Nor is it an esoteric art form practiced by temperamental geniuses. You don't learn to write by enrolling in an MFA program in a university. Writing is a craft. You learn it the same way you learn any other craft, whether it's flying, cooking, or woodworking: by application and experiment.

Which means that writers *write*. It's that simple distinction that separates most aspiring but never published writers from those who succeed. Unsuccessful writers talk about writing. They make occasional forays at it. They complain about writer's block. They get around to writing when they have time. They write when inspiration strikes.

Successful writers don't wait until they have time. They don't have writer's block, nor do they wait for inspiration's kiss. Successful writers understand that writer's block is a myth. They've learned exactly when inspiration presents itself: at the moment they plant themselves at their desks and go to work.

But there's more. Sheer output of written words is not enough. It's possible—and altogether common—for aspiring writers to crank out hundreds of thousands of words . . . and never improve. They never produce publishable work because they don't change. They never break out of their original and ineffective writing style.

To advance as a writer you must be willing to experiment, to try out different styles, voices, techniques. Just as an emerging artist or musician or actor learns by emulating the masters in their field, so does the writer. Does this voice work for you? If not, why not? Which point of view is most effective? Third person singular? First person? Try them all. Do terse, bullet point sentences fit your writing better than a sonorous, embellished style? Try them out. Compare them. By this means—reading, emulating, experimenting—you're closing in on the special style and voice that is yours.

And where do you find these other styles to emulate? By reading. The act of reading is as natural to a writer as breathing. Successful writers read voraciously. They read in a multiplicity of genres and styles. They read not just for the appreciation of literature, but to understand *why* certain writing stands out from the rest. They analyze authors' voices, searching for the inflections and styles and nuances that distinguish good writing from bad.

Should you postpone your writing mission until you think you've mastered the craft? Certainly not. Just keep in mind that writing, like every mission, is an ongoing *learning* experience. Yes, you'll make your book the best product you possibly can, but what you learn from the experience you apply to your *next* writing mission. And the next. Each incremental step will lead you to a higher plateau in your development as a writer.

One day, somewhere in the course of your mission, you'll make a remarkable discovery. Your writing is different. It has a clarity and quality that weren't there before. You're writing in a voice that is unique to you.

Take a moment to congratulate yourself. You've come a great distance. You've passed a critical waypoint in your mission. And having basked this short while in the glow of your accomplishment, do what must be done next: return to your mission.

Stay committed.

Writing: the Business

Sir, nobody but a blockhead ever wrote except for money.
– SAMUEL JOHNSON

There are few enterprises more entrepreneurial than the business of writing. The writer/entrepreneur is the envisioner of the product, the creative director, the chief marketer, the CEO of the business. If the writer doesn't produce, she doesn't earn. If the writer doesn't have ideas, she doesn't have a business. The product, if there is to be one, comes from the writer's imagination. Whether the business soars or never leaves the ground depends entirely on the writer's efforts.

Does that seem daunting? Perhaps, but it's also hugely empowering. In few other business activities do you have so much control. Or opportunity. Never has it been more possible for the emerging writer/entrepreneur to create, publish, and market a product.

It was not always so. For most of the past two centuries, which is to say the *old* publishing paradigm, the business was controlled by legacy publishers. The large New York publishing houses were the curators and gatekeepers of the American public's reading material. And positioned between authors and publishers was yet another legion of gatekeepers—the literary agents. It was a joke and a classic Catch 22: you couldn't be published unless you had an agent, and you couldn't get an agent unless you'd been published.

In the old paradigm, advances paid by publishers tended to be generous. Agents and authors negotiated big advances, the idea being that the more eye-watering the advance, the more incentive the publisher had to promote the book.

Also in the old paradigm, the assigned duties were neatly segregated. Writers wrote books, publishers sold them. Once an author finished writing a book, all the production details were handled by the publisher—copyediting, proofreading, formatting, layout, jacket design. So was all the marketing, which included advertising, soliciting reviews and blurbs, and a glitzy author's tour.

Then came the perfect storm. The computer age, the internet, and the arrival of the 8,000-pound gorilla called Amazon converged to change forever how books were produced, marketed, and read. It was the most profound change in publishing since the Gutenberg press. Even the definition of "book" was transformed. New handheld devices, multi-media formats, and interactive displays changed the very nature of literary content.

In this post-storm publishing world, emerging writers no longer have to pass the gatekeepers. Books can be packaged, published, marketed, and distributed *without* agents or legacy publishers. Which means that you, the writer/entrepreneur, are on your own. In this brave new world you receive no advance against royalties, no copyediting or formatting, no marketing. Everything is on your account, including the book tour.

What has this storm done to the legacy publishers? Many of the proud old names—William Morrow, E. F. Hutton, Putnam,

Penguin—have been forced to merge into a handful of conglomerates. Gone is the old publishing model, wherein editors evaluated books and offered advances based on books' quality. For today's publishers it's all about *platform*, meaning how does the *author* intend to sell the proposed book? What reviews will the *author* obtain? How big a readership will the *author* attract? If the book is published, how will the *author* promote it?

Gone too are most of the old perks. The author's book tour? Forget it—unless the author pays for it. Advertising? On the author's tab. Reviews and blurbs? It's the author's job to obtain them. And what happened to that big advance? *Poof!* Vaporized along with the other publisher-paid perks. Mid-list authors—the majority of the writers being published—receive a paltry advance up front and then must wait for the royalties to roll in from actual book sales.

Ah, yes, the royalties. That's one artifact from the legacy era that hasn't changed. The author's share of book proceeds remains where it has always been—somewhere between 12 percent and 15 percent of a book's selling price, further reduced by the agent's commission of 15 percent.

How does that compare to royalties in the world of independent publishing? Amazon currently pays authors a 70 percent royalty for eBook sales in its U. S. Kindle store. Online marketers such as Nook (the publishing arm of Barnes&Noble) and Smashwords (iBooks, Sony, Kobo, B&N, and others) offer comparable royalties. Audible.com pays up to 40 percent to authors of audio books. CreateSpace, a print-on-demand subsidiary of Amazon, computes a royalty based on the book's list price, printing charges, and sales channel charges. The typical royalty for a 184-page book listed at $8.99 amounts to $2.34, or 26 percent.

Given this disparity in royalty share, why would an author choose to publish via a legacy publisher? One time-honored reason is *cachet*. Being published by a legacy publisher still carries a stamp of distinction. The publisher's imprint signals that the book—and its author—have been curated by the establishment gatekeepers and deemed acceptable. The book will find a placement on the shelves of brick-and-mortar bookstores. A fortunate few will receive thoughtful reviews in newspapers like the *New York Times*. For a rising new author such cachet has undeniable value.

But neither publishing route—legacy or independent—is a one-way street. Many writers who have found success publishing independently have made the jump to mainstream publishing. And numerous established writers have opted out of mainstream publishing contracts to market their books independently. Bestseller lists are becoming populated by writers from both worlds.

What are you, an emerging writer/entrepreneur, to make of this? Instead of a *new* publishing paradigm, you have a *changing* paradigm. To survive and prosper in this free-for-all new paradigm, you have to stay in synch with the evolving new tools: social media, blogs, authors' web sites, email lists, search engine optimization. As quickly as a new marketing or publishing tool becomes an industry standard, a newer one appears.

Which means you must be nimble. Willing to learn. Ready to adapt. And, most of all, believe in your writing mission.

> *People on the outside think there's something magical about writing, that you go up in the attic at midnight and cast the bones and come down in the morning with a story, but it isn't like that. You sit in back of the typewriter and you work, and that's all there is to it.*
> —HARLAN ELLISON

The Steps of a Writing Mission

— **Select the project:** Identify your genre. Memoir, novel, history, how-to book?

— **Define the objective:** Print edition, e-book, audio? Identify your target audience. Determine your publishing medium. Legacy publisher via an agent? Or self-publish either through a subsidy publisher or on your own.

— **Do the research:** A memoir will probably be drawn from your sources—diaries, photos, yearbooks, your own memory. Any kind of history will be preceded by a study of your subject and era. Your novel, even if it's drawn entirely from imagination, should be fleshed out in your mind and on paper—characters, story arc, theme.

— **Apply a time frame:** Pick a number of words you expect to write each working day. Estimate the size of your book. Do the math, allow half again as much time for the rewriting and editing. Set a target time.

— **Commit:** The most essential of steps. Only by applying your full commitment will you get through the valleys and speed bumps and sinkholes that attend every worthwhile writing project.

The writing mission isn't for everyone. It can be a lonely pursuit, facing a blank screen each morning, searching for ideas in empty space, giving life to scenes and characters and stories that exist only in your imagination. The passion that drove you to undertake the mission may fade. Your commitment may falter.

How do you maintain that original commitment? The same way you stay committed to any mission: By being persistent. By sticking to your mission plan. By keeping a written log of your progress toward your destination. By visualizing the benefits that will flow from your accomplishment.

Perhaps the sweetest benefit will come one day when you pause at your keyboard and gaze with astonishment at what you see. A realization strikes you like a thunderclap. *Something extraordinary has happened.* That nearly forgotten dream that moldered all those years in the secret trove? You've dusted it off and dragged into the sunlight. It's a reality. You're living that dream.

You're a writer.

Part Six

Embracing the New

Do stuff. Be clenched, curious. Not waiting for inspiration's shove or society's kiss on your forehead... Pay attention... Attention is vitality. It connects you with others. It makes you eager. Stay eager.
                    —SUSAN SONTAG

26

Do *What*? At *My* Age?

An object at rest stays at rest, and an object in motion stays in motion with the same speed and in the same direction unless acted upon by an unbalanced force.
—NEWTON'S FIRST LAW OF MOTION

Newton's first law describes inertia, and it applies to people just as it does to inanimate objects. In behavioral language, Newton's law means that people tend to keep on doing what they're doing—or not doing—unless some force causes them to change. That force can come from within or without. In the case of senior adults it may require a willful decision—a metaphorical Newtonian force—to overcome decades of not doing.

One of the results of those decades is the nearly imperceptible erosion of your confidence. Via the media, your peers, and—worst of all—your own privately held notions, you become conditioned to believe that your ability to learn diminishes with age. Like an incessant drumbeat, you hear the subliminal whispers flitting through your brain . . .

— *Who, me? Learn to play the piano NOW?*

— *Learn Italian at MY age?*

— *Learn to fly, skateboard, dance the Tango, write a software program. . . NO WAY!*

— *I'm TOO OLD to . . .* [Fill in the blank].

The subliminal whispers are not only dead wrong, they're deadly. The whispers—and their underlying message—become a self-fulfilling prophecy. Each repetition of the message removes another chink from your self-confidence. In tiny increments you conclude that the effort to learn a new subject is futile. Why waste precious time trying to learn something that you immediately forget?

And what happens to your brain when you cease learning? The effect is analogous to what happens to your body when you forego physical exercise. Atrophy sets in. Little by little, day by day, you forfeit pieces of your mental or physical power.

That's the bad news. The good news is that the condition is reversible. Just as an out-of-shape body can be returned to an active, vital state, so can your brain. Is it easy? Of course not. Is it worth it? Emphatically yes. But only if you are willing to put in the effort.

Where to begin? As usual. With an assessment.

Evolving Reality

One of the fundamental requirements of Mastery is that you confront the truth. No rose-colored glasses, no blinders, no obscuring the real nature of your world. It means recognizing the evolving reality of your mind, your body, your time—and making the most of them. It also means not deluding yourself by pretending that the workings of your brain and body haven't altered over the years.

But there is a far worse delusion. It's the notion that age has erased your capacity for growth and learning. The erroneous belief that you can no longer expand your potential—physical or mental— may be the most spirit-draining and deadly of all delusions.

True, your physical capabilities are not the same as when you were twenty or thirty. That's evolving reality. It's also true that you may not master new subjects—languages, music, art forms— the same way you did when you were young. And that's not all bad. You have the ability to learn new subjects just as you always did— but you learn in a different way. In some ways you are *better* equipped to learn than when you were younger. Learning has taken a different direction and urgency than when you were an undirected and unhurried youth.

As a seeker of Mastery, you possess an important advantage: you know that life is finite. You appreciate the exquisite importance of NOW. You choose to act on your plans instead of waiting until sometime in the fuzzy future. That language you want to speak? The dance step that you promised yourself you'd master? The computer code you intend to learn? They're within your grasp. The time to seize them is now.

Applying the principles of Mastery doesn't mean that you reverse the effects of time. Nor does it mean that you suspend the rules of physics and physiology. It means that you recognize the evolving reality of your most precious assets, and you intend to make the most of them. Armed with this knowledge, you are poised to learn like never before.

Profiles in Mastery

I. F. Stone

Journalist I. F. "Izzy" Stone was a troublemaker. He was an investigative reporter and author who for half a century managed to rankle politicians and bureaucrats on all sides of the political spectrum. His newsletter, the Weekly, *made him an influential figure in Washington.*

Stone was also a ceaseless learner and pursuer of missions. When he became seriously ill in his seventies, he ceased publication of his newsletter. Instead of entering retirement, he returned to the University of Pennsylvania where he had dropped out in his youth. He became a student, earning the bachelor's degree that had eluded him half a century before.

As Stone's health continued to decline, he became hospitalized. Friends and wellwishers came to pay their last respects. They were surprised to see the stack of Greek language books on the dying man's nightstand. Greek? What in the world for?

It was his new mission, Stone informed them. He was going to learn ancient Greek.

Visitors exchanged glances. Umm, that was nice, but why . . . now? Stone informed them that he wanted to read untranslated works in the original language because he intended to write a book about ancient Greece. It was a subject that had long interested him.

credit: Sandra Strait

His friends nodded politely. They wished him well.

And then more surprises. Izzy Stone didn't die as expected. He pursued his mission. He did learn classical Greek, learning it well enough to read the ancient tracts in their original language, just as he intended. And then, also as intended, he wrote his twelfth book, The Trial of Socrates, *which was published to much critical acclaim.*

And he kept writing. For several more years Izzy Stone continued on the path to Mastery, learning, growing, surprising friends and critics until his death at age eighty-one.

Learn a Language

The more languages you know, the more you are human.
— TOMÁŠ GARRIGUE MASARYK

Polyglots like Benny Lewis[1] and Gabriel Wyner[2] have proven that learning a second or third foreign language is easier than learning the first. They know that language learning builds on itself. Your brain, in effect, rewires itself when you become multilingual, forming new circuitry.[3]

But learning another language or a musical instrument or a new motor skill from scratch can be a rocky path. Memorizing a new vocabulary, struggling with a seemingly incomprehensible grammar, repeating the same fumble-fingered mistakes on a keyboard—these minor challenges become a cumulative discouragement. Three steps forward, two back.

To preserve your enthusiasm, take smaller steps. Too many adult students of language or music or technical skills commence their studies in a burst of euphoria, then hit a wall of discouragement before reaching their first goal.

There are multiple ways to acquire a new language. It can be done in a class, on a computer, or interactively with a tutor or even by alternating tutoring with a foreign language speaker who wants to learn English.

Here's an example. Let's say your mission is to learn Spanish. As with all missions in Mastery, you begin with a plan. Be realistic, define your objectives, and—this is important—apply a timeframe.

Your mission plan would look something like this:

— **Objective:** to speak conversationally, read and write intermediate level, understand basic spoken Spanish.

— **Strategy**

(1) Take a course appropriate for your level (Rosetta Stone, Pimsleur, local class—pick one).

(2) Retain a tutor or coach for conversational training. This works well if your coach encourages you to think and interact in the new language. Make the sessions short but frequent. Alternatively, engage an on-line tutor. Or find a Spanish-speaker who wants to swap English training for Spanish.

(3) Immerse in the language—no English—in a Spanish-speaking environment. Make it a travel destination where you can absorb not only your new language but a fresh culture.

— **Waypoints:**

(1) Acquire basic grammar and 3000-word vocabulary. Do this in digestible parcels. For example, using Anki or another spaced repetition system, learn ten new words per day—or a number you can handle without being overwhelmed—while reinforcing the words you recently learned.

(2) Attain read/write capability.

(3) Reach basic conversational skill with native speaker.

— **Time frame:** Six months for basic vocabulary, grammar, and read/write proficiency. One year (including immersion session) to reach basic fluency.

This is a simplified plan. You will certainly apply specifics to your own language learning mission. But with every mission plan, whether it's learning a language, the piano, or kick boxing, you'll follow this general format.

What's the toughest part of language learning? For almost everyone, regardless of age, it's remembering what you've learned. To acquire any new language, you must learn thousands of vocabulary words, conjugations of verbs, idioms peculiar to the language.

Then comes the hard part. You must *retain* all that information. For many adult students, *that* becomes the deal breaker.

But it needn't be. Part of Mastery is learning how to learn—and learning how to retain what you learn. Here's a way.

Spaced Repetition Learning

With the arrival of Google and the Internet and smart devices, you hear an increasingly common question: *Why should I have to remember dry facts? Everything I need to know is accessible on line.*

Could it be that remembering words, dates, place names, historical details is no longer relevant? Isn't it true that every fact, data point, and word definition will soon be available on a handheld tablet?

Is memorization obsolete?

Only to wishful thinkers. The reality is that almost all linguistic, scientific, and artistic skills require memorization. *Lots* of memorization, which, for many students, is immediately followed by *lots* of forgetting.

The retention problem is real, and it's one of the main reasons adults shun learning new skills—language, music, art. Why put in countless hours of your life memorizing hundreds of words and phrases only to see your efforts evaporate like melting snow?

The problem is not unique to older students. Studies show that human forgetting follows a pattern. If your data retention rate were plotted on a graph, you'd see your grip on precious newly learned information dropping like a stone within hours of having acquired it. This is why those all-nighters you put in cramming for an exam produced a passing grade the next day—but left you clueless for the same answers a week later.

Fortunately, there's a better way to learn—and to retain what you learn. It's called spaced repetition, and it has the potential to revolutionize how students—young and old—acquire and remember material. Spaced repetition systems work on the concept that active recall is far more effective than simply rereading the same information. Active recall is triggered by what psychologists call the "testing effect."

"To this day," says Robert Bjork, chair of UCLA's psychology department, "most people think about forgetting as decay, that memories are like footprints in the sand that gradually fade away. But that has been disproved by a lot of research. The memory appears to be gone because you can't recall it, but we can prove that it's still there. For instance, you can still recognize a 'forgotten' item in a group. Yes, without continued use, things become inaccessible. But they are not gone."[4]

Francis Bacon described the testing effect centuries ago: "If you read a piece of text through twenty times, you will not learn it by heart so easily as if you read it ten times while attempting to recite from time to time and consulting the text when your memory fails." This means that testing yourself on newly learned information gives you a far stronger likelihood of retaining it than by simply rereading it.

But the timing of the test is crucial. Studies show that the best time to test recall is at the point when you've almost forgotten the information. It's the effort to recall nearly-forgotten data that actually locks it into your memory. The closer you are to forgetting an item, the better it will stick in your memory when you finally remember it. The time-honored exam-preparation technique of reading and rereading information prior to a test provides quick early recall but results in a far lower retention of the data than if you read it only once, were tested, then after an interval in time were tested again.

The challenge with spaced repetition learning is determining *when* to test your recall. If the intervals between testing are correctly spaced, they have a powerful effect on your long term retention. The ability to re-expose your memory to the snippets at spaced intervals provides a potent new tool for locking in the information.

A spaced repetition system is an ideal technique for memory-intensive subjects like languages, science, and history. But how to tailor an SRS to your chosen subject?

Flash cards have long been the tool of choice for testing and retaining snippets of information. But constructing an SRS system with flashcards—a phrase or question on one side and the answer on the other— was labor intensive and imprecise. It required creating multiple stacks of cards sorted by intervals between testing sessions and by how well you recalled each item.

Then came the digital age. New computer-based flashcard systems have arrived that determine the best interval between test repetitions for each card. Based on algorithms that determine how far into the future to send your newly learned information, you learn, almost forget, reinforce what you learned. An SRS can mean the end of wasting your time learning and then forgetting long lists of vocabulary words and grammar usages. That information will become stored in your memory permanently.

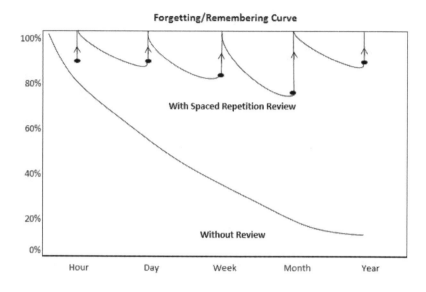

Forgetting/Remembering Curve

credit: Sandra Strait

An SRS works like this: Your daily study session may cover thirty new vocabulary words or phrases. During each successive session, you'll learn new words, plus you'll be tested on old words you learned before. You tell the system whether you recalled the word easily, with difficulty, or not at all, and the system reintroduces the word to you at the correct time in the future. During any session you'll be learning new words as well as recalling old ones you have nearly forgotten.

Several computerized SRSs are available, including SuperMemo, Mnemosyne, and Anki. Of these, the most complex is SuperMemo, the pioneering system developed in the '80s by Polish researcher Piotr Woźniak. SuperMemo runs on Windows and IOS platforms. Mnemosyne and Anki are open source programs available on Mac as well as Windows and are easy to set up. While the desktop version of Anki is free, it synchs with the Apple iPhone and iPad and Android apps and, like Mnemosyne, can be accessed via any web browser.

For those who resist digital tools, you can create your own SRS with physical flash cards. A Leitner box, named after an Austrian science journalist, works the same way as a digital SRS. For your manual SRS, you need a set of flash cards, dividers, and a calendar. In the basic version, the cards are divided into four sections. Section one gets reviewed every day, section two every two days, and each subsequent section after four or more days. Each time you easily recall a card, it advances to the next section. When you forget a card, it goes back to section one.

Profiles in Mastery

Piotr Wozniak

Depending on your point of view, Piotr Wozniak is either a colorful eccentric or a supreme example of Mastery. The Polish developer of <u>SuperMemo</u>, *the pioneering flashcard-based spaced repetition learning system, is also a polymath who has made a career of mastering a myriad of subjects.*

Wozniak speaks nearly perfect English though he's never traveled to an English-speaking country. He learned it the same way he learns most subjects—using his own spaced repetition system. Wozniak's personal data base contains hundreds of thousands of memory items, which he spends several hours per day reviewing. His day is divided into slots, each devoted to one of his many passions—language study, sports, reading, sleeping, or one of his ongoing experiments with memory and task management programs.

Wozniak's own life is an ongoing experiment. A few years ago he ditched his alarm clock to adopt what he called "free running sleep." He sleeps when he feels sleepy, and wakes up when his body is ready. Such a schedule, of course, doesn't accommodate a normal social life, which matters little to Wozniak. He is famously uncontactable, ignoring telephones, email, doorbells, going to ground for weeks at a time while embarked on one of his missions of learning.

Early in his academic career in Poland, Wozniak, who holds a Ph.D. from the University of Economics in Wroclaw, observed that most students retained knowledge of their subjects just long enough to pass their exams. Within months of completing a class, only a fraction of that hard-earned education was still accessible. Finding a better way to learn became Piotr Wozniak's mission.

Wozniak was convinced that computers, given the right algorithm, could calculate the precise moment of forgetting any newly learned item or fact. By correctly spacing the intervals between moments of nearly forgetting, Wozniak's SuperMemo (and most other spaced repetition systems) can lock information—languages, scientific formulas, facts of history—into your brain, ready for retrieval.

Wozniak's missions (or eccentricities) extend beyond the cerebral. To the Baltic Sea, for example. Dark and frigid, the Baltic holds a peculiar attraction for Wozniak. In mid-winter, parka-wearing walkers are startled at the sight of the tall, athletically-built man in shorts jogging along the shore. Stunned, they watch him veer toward the sea and plunge headlong into the icy Baltic. After several minutes of swimming the man emerges from the surf . . . and resumes jogging.

credit: Sandra Strait

For Piotr Wozniak, it's a routine day at the beach. Defying the hypothermia-inducing effect of freezing seawater is as much a mental accomplishment as physical. Just another mission on Wozniak's route to Mastery.

The Juggling Mission

The use-it-or-lose-it imperative applies to the brain just as it does to the body. Not only can old dogs learn new tricks, they *have to* keep learning in order to retain their capabilities. Just as unused muscles atrophy, so does the brain. What this means to the seeker of Mastery is that acquiring new skills and fresh knowledge is not a leisure activity. It's a way of life.

Learning begets learning. Linguists know that the time required to learn a foreign language becomes progressively shorter with the addition of each new language. The marvelous plasticity of the brain manifests itself in ways you would not expect. The process of learning a motor skill or acquiring new knowledge stimulates the brain's receptivity to acquiring additional new skills. Something magical happens each time you accomplish a new mission. Your confidence grows. Your potential as an advanced human being expands exponentially. A quiet pride swells within you.

And so it is with the mission of juggling.

Juggling? Wouldn't that seem to be a . . . trivial pursuit? Why should anyone invest the time and energy in something as unproductive as tossing and catching a few balls?

We're glad you asked. Here are a few good reasons why you should learn to juggle:

— **Juggling improves coordination.**

>Few of us are ambidextrous, which is the key element of juggling. After learning to juggle you may discover that you've acquired a new hand-eye facility that you never thought possible. Even highly coordinated athletes have taken their hand-eye skills to a new level by juggling.

— **Juggling induces a state of relaxed concentration.**

>When your mind is occupied in a rhythmic mind-body exercise like juggling, you are prepared to enter the detached, ethereal condition called the Zone. At this stage juggling becomes effortless, the balls seeming to juggle themselves.

— **Juggling boosts your brain power.**

266

A study conducted at the University of Regensberg concluded that learning to juggle caused certain areas of their subjects' brains to grow. But the most significant finding was that *learning* a new skill did more to change the brain's structure than simply continuing the practice of an already-learned task. [5]

— **Juggling relaxes you.**

When you are learning to juggle, your mind is fully absorbed in the activity. Your sources of stress, worry, preoccupation with business all fade into the background. Studies with control groups have shown that juggling is an effective therapy for stress and anxiety.[6]

— **Juggling increases the range of motion in the arms and shoulders.**

The process of juggling lubricates critical joints by gently exercising them in directions they seldom move.

And of course, perhaps the most important . . .

— **Juggling is fun.**

The missing ingredient in many otherwise productive lives is the child-like ability to indulge in play. The very act of immersing yourself in a non-serious but engaging activity like juggling has a liberating effect.

Learning to Juggle

You can begin with commonplace objects—oranges, tennis balls, potatoes—but consider investing in a basic set of three Schylling juggling balls. The vinyl-covered balls are soft enough not to bounce (yes, you'll be dropping them—a lot), are cheap, and pack easily for trips. You can also begin the learning process by using scarves instead of balls. They're easier to catch, and because the routine seems to take place in slow motion, it allows you to get the picture before moving on to the balls.

— Focus on the toss

Think about those occasions when someone tossed you something you didn't expect—and your hand reflexively caught the object. Juggling is all about tossing. By focusing on tossing consistently, the catching will take care of itself. Your goal is to toss each ball in a forehead-high arc from one hand to the other. It will help to visualize a box. The top plane of the box is a few inches above your head. Your hands and forearms rest at the bottom of the box. Your goal is to toss the ball from your right hand to the upper left-of-center plane of the box and the left hand ball to the right of center. Hit each of these targets, and the ball will naturally fall into the opposite hand.

Toss one ball

— Holding the ball in your right hand, toss the ball in an arc slightly above and to the left of your head.

— Catch the ball with your left hand.

— Repeat, tossing the same ball with your left hand to the opposite point above and to the right of your head.

— Continue this practice while you pay attention to your breathing, posture, and eye focus. It helps to "soft focus"— letting your eyes relax and *not* fix on the ascending and descending balls. Let your expanded peripheral vision take over, and your hands will instinctively find the right position. Flex your wrists and forearms in easy, fluid motions.

— If your toss goes astray, *let the ball drop*. Remind yourself that it's all about the toss, not the catch. During your one-ball practice, try to find a smooth rhythm for your tosses.

Toss two balls

— Holding a ball in each hand, toss the right ball to the same point slightly over your head and to the left. When the ball reaches its peak, toss the ball in your left hand up and to the right.

— Catch the first ball in your left hand. Then catch the second ball in your right hand. If either ball goes astray, let it drop.

— Repeat, this time starting the tosses from your left hand. Catch each ball. If either is off target, let it drop.

— Stop, smile, and congratulate yourself.

— Resume practicing until you can keep the two balls ascending and descending in a pleasing rhythm.

Graduate to three balls

— The tosses and catches with three balls are exactly the same as with one and two balls. You may not feel ready for this because you're still dropping balls in the two-ball routine. No matter. Just remind yourself that pushing your envelope and stretching your capability is how you grow.

— Holding two balls in your right hand and one in the left, toss one of the balls in your right hand. When it reaches its apex, toss the ball in your left hand, just as you did in the two-ball exercise. When that ball reaches its highest point, toss the ball you just caught in your right hand.

— When you have caught each of the three balls, you have performed your first three-ball jugulation.

— Stop. Smile again. Bask in the glory of your accomplishment.

— Resume practice. Continue tossing the balls, trying to keep the jugulation going. Keep your attention on tossing the balls accurately, and the rest will follow. Yes, you'll be stopping often to pick up balls. Just remember that this is part of the learning—and the fun. Relax and enjoy the process.

There are multiple sources for instruction in juggling. A valuable site for DVDs and books, juggling balls and rings, and on-line demos is the World Juggling Federation. Another is "Learn How to Juggle Now!" at JuggleFit.com. In his book *More Balls Than Hands*, author Michael Gelb offers not only a step-by-step tutorial, he brilliantly describes the Zen-like freedom of losing yourself in the simple flow of juggling.

In the overall concept of Mastery, a mission such as learning to juggle may seem inconsequential. Remember that missions come in all sizes, all levels of effort. What makes any mission worthwhile, whether it's juggling, learning a language, starting a business, is your level of commitment. Real success requires setting goals, recording your progress, visualizing results.

Learning to juggle may be seen as a metaphor for *all* the missions you undertake in the future. It is this essential skill—your marvelous power to learn—that will fuel your progress toward Mastery.

---

1   Benny Lewis is a fun-loving Irishman and globe-trotter. He's also fluent in seven languages, and promotes his own system for learning foreign languages. He runs a web site and blog at http://www.fluentin3months.com.

2   Gabriel Wyner is the author of a best-selling book, *Fluent Forever,* in which he describes in detail how to construct an Anki flashcard system based on spaced repetition learning. He has a useful web site at https://fluent-forever.com

3   People who are bilingual have an advantage over the rest of us, and not just in terms of communication skills, according to researcher Andrea Mechelli, who believes the bilingual brain develops more densely, giving it an advantage in various abilities and skills. "Our findings suggest that the structure of the human brain is altered by the experience of acquiring a second language," wrote Mechelli in the October 2004 issue of the journal *Nature.*

4   Piotr Wozniak, developer of the spaced repetition system called SuperMemo, exemplifies the principles of

Mastery. According to writer Gary Wolf in *Wired*, "Wozniak takes an almost physical pleasure in reason. He loves to discuss things with people, to get insight into their personalities, and to give them advice — especially in English. One of his most heartfelt wishes is that the world have one language and one currency so this could all be handled more efficiently. He's appalled that Poland is still not in the Eurozone. He's baffled that Americans do not use the metric system. For two years he kept a diary in Esperanto."

5 Dr. Arne May, who led the study on juggling and gray matter, reported, "It suggests that learning a skill is more important than exercising what you are good at already – the brain wants to be puzzled and learn something new."

6 A National Institutes of Health report entitled "Effect of juggling therapy on anxiety disorders in female patients" found in a control group of 17 patients that, after six months, tension anxiety was significantly reduced in those undergoing juggling therapy.

27

Technology

There is only one thing for it then—to learn. Learn why the world wags and what wags it. That is the only thing which the mind can never exhaust, never alienate, never be tortured by, never fear or distrust, and never dream of regretting.
  —T. H. WHITE, *The Once and Future King.*

The pace of change in the world is accelerating. Technology, art, communication, life styles—all are evolving at a dizzying rate. A demarcation has emerged not just between generations— Boomers, Pre-Boomers, Millennials, Gen-Xers—but between participants and spectators on the modern playing field.

How many seniors do you know who are intimidated by computers, by the internet, by smart phones and tablets? How many believe that technology has passed them by? That it's too late for them to learn the complexities of the tech world?

For many, this wrong-headed thinking will become reality. The world *will* pass them by. And needlessly so.

Thus another hard truth: *By not continuing to learn, the more difficult it becomes to learn.* But there's a flip side to that truth. *The more you learn, the easier it becomes to learn.* We've discussed this before—the phenomenon called neuroplasticity. The pure cognitive exercise of learning any new skill changes your brain, adapting it for more learning tasks.

For seniors this is a singularly powerful concept. "To keep the brain fit," says Dr. Norman Doidge, author of *The Brain That Changes Itself*, "we must learn something new rather than simply replaying already-mastered skills."

Learning begets learning.

And so it is with technology. Regardless of how you feel about computer science and the virtual world to which it connects you, it is a force driving the future of your world. Health care, finance, transportation—almost every essential facet of your life—is being transformed by technology.

And yes, you may choose to opt out. For perfectly valid reasons you may decide that the world can continue to evolve without you. You're content with the devices and culture from an era of your choosing. You've experienced enough change, thank you, and you prefer to focus your attention inward. Your personal growth will come from another source.

Fair enough. Certainly, inner growth can be achieved without joining the hubbub and furor of the outside world.

But consider again. Take a moment to reflect on another aspect of personal growth. Consider the kind of growth that comes from *embracing* the newness of your evolving world. The kind you experience by being open to change and innovation. The kind of growth that comes not just from exposure to a new culture, but from active involvement. It's that curious, hands-on, under-the-hood tinkering mentality that precedes discovery— the transformational moment when you reach a new plateau of knowledge. It's the kind of growth you experienced as a child when *everything* was new and your brain was filled with questions.

By keeping abreast of technology, you profit in two ways. As technology transforms the world you live in, you are part of it. You are participating in the rapid advances in science, health care, and business. As an example, consider how the internet and its plethora of e-business opportunities have spawned a new wave of entrepreneurs. As a participant in this wave, you are positioned to spot rich new opportunities generated by modern technology. You can start an online business, write a newsletter, publish a book. The list of opportunities is growing exponentially. Best of all, in this virtual new world there are no age limits.

Technology is the great equalizer.

The second way you profit is more abstract. The exercise of learning a new subject, whether it's photography, or digital publishing, or a computer program, has a life-enhancing effect. It not only stimulates your brain—the plasticity effect—it keeps you in the game. You have the sense of being engaged with the evolving world. You have a connection not only to other generations but to other cultures. By mastering any form of new technology, you receive the satisfaction of having given yourself a worthy mission—and executing it.

As a mature adult, you can have the best of two worlds. You already possess a storehouse of knowledge about legacy skills—everything from stick shift autos to manual typewriters to ham radio. To these you can add a whole new world of modern cutting edge digital skills. Think of it as learning to drive while your 19th century peers are still on horseback.

Technology is the leveler of the modern playing field.

At this point you may be shaking your head. It's just not that easy, you're thinking. When you're coming from behind on an ever-steepening technology slope, it's tough to catch up.

Tough, yes, but you might not be as far behind as you think. There are myriad ways you can become knowledgeable about modern devices. For starters, you can make it your habit to read the personal tech columns in your newspapers and periodicals. You can stay abreast of ongoing new developments in consumer electronics. You can sign up for a computer or internet class offered at one of your local schools or colleges. You can check out the many online tutorials for applications such as word processing, mail handling, spread sheets, data bases, photo processing, or basic computer literacy. Learning sites such as <u>Alison</u>, <u>Meganga</u>, and <u>Home and Learn</u> offer tutorials in everything from beginning computer skills to advanced programming language. For Mac OSX system users, there are dedicated sites such as <u>MacComputerLessons</u> and <u>PC Classes Online</u>. Apple retail stores provide a variety of workshops on all the Apple computers and handheld devices. Many of the learning sites also offer instruction in hand held devices—iPhone, iPad, and Android phones and tablets.

Make your goal of learning technology an authentic mission. Just as with any other mission, give it a plan, a series of objectives and waypoints, and a time frame. Your reward will be empowerment in the coming age of abundance.

New Times, New Ideas

When the facts change, I change my mind. What do you do, sir?
—Economist JOHN MAYNARD KEYNES, when criticized for
having been inconsistent in his position.

You've experienced this scenario. You're engaged in a heated discussion with someone. You *know* you're right, they're wrong, and it takes all your patience to wait for them to finish speaking. You hear little of what they are saying because your mind is occupied planning your own next statement.

And somewhere in the discourse it happens. You miss something. Something important.

Had you paid more attention, listened with an open mind, you might have caught the nuance in the other's argument that cast the issue in a wholly different light.

When was the last time you reexamined your beliefs about some of the hot button issues of our time? How open are you to fresh ideas that conflict with your own long-held beliefs? How willing are you to engage in discourse with people of opposing viewpoints? To what extent do you actually *listen* to their positions?

How likely is it that you would change your mind as a result of such a discussion?

Not likely, perhaps. You wouldn't be expected to change any of your long held beliefs, religious or secular, in the space of a conversation. Nor should you consider shifting your ethics or values to accommodate changing times. What you should do, however, is try viewing yourself and your world from a detached point of view. As an experiment, try making yourself an impartial, open-minded observer of your world and the people around you.

Which requires paying attention. *Real* attention. When you actually listen to the argument of someone with an opinion different from yours, you gain a unique perspective—and advantage. Instead of waiting until you can insert your own point of view, try *actively* listening. Being a *receptor* instead of a transmitter. By allowing your mind to absorb and comprehend what the speaker is saying, you not only show respect, you empower yourself. You are being proactive, seizing an opportunity to learn—and thus to grow.

This is Mastery in its purest form. By keeping all your faculties receptive to the world around you, you continue to evolve as an advanced human being.

Young Friends, Old Friends

Something happens in later life. You saw it when you were growing up— grandparents, great uncles and aunts, elderly neighbors—all cluttering their houses with the accumulated brickabrack of a bygone age. You remember smiling at their unwillingness to adopt new gadgets. You observed their befuddlement with everything from VCRs to the Beatles to TV remotes. Their circle of friends narrowed, consisting of people their own age. Their conversation dwelled on events in the past. You thought they were out of touch. Stuck in the past.

That was then. This is now, and it's time for another assessment. Look around you. How many new friends have *you* made lately? How many are your age? How many are younger?

How receptive are you to emerging technology—smart devices, social media, artificial intelligence, 3D printers? What are your sources for news, entertainment, financial and technological information?

Like many people, you may have become less gregarious as you've grown older. You may be less willing to interact with strangers, particularly strangers of a different age and ilk than you. Meeting new friends seems problematic. Striking up relationships with strangers, particularly strangers of a different generation whose attitudes and lifestyles are in stark contrast to your own, encroaches on your comfort zone.

You're not alone. In tiny increments over the years, older people erect a fence around their private world with a sign: *Access Permitted Only For People Like Me.* They migrate to retirement colonies where they can blend in with like-minded, inertia-bound oldsters.

And no, that's not all bad. There are huge benefits to living in a community especially attuned to the needs of older citizens. But for many such residents, these cloistered settlements become a trap. Sealed off from other generations and cultures, the inhabitants retreat into their own shells.

Thus the challenge: how to stay engaged with members of other age groups and interests. Just as travel provides the opportunity to meet new and interesting friends, so do most learning experiences. Whether it's Tai Chi, the French language, or free style swimming, most learning experiences provide a built-in engagement with instructors, staff, other students. Group clinics, meetings, forums should be opportunities to interact.

But the value in acquiring new friends of all ages extends beyond just the pleasure of companionship. Your perspective changes as you expand the breadth and scope of your acquaintances. Just as travel has the power to transform you by opening you up to new ideas and cultures, so does the experience of making new friends.

Let curiosity continue to be a driving force in your life. Ask questions. Let the same sense of awe that draws you to panoramas like Machu Picchu or the Grand Canyon lead you to rewarding new friendships—young and old.

ROBERT GANDT AND GARY A. SCOTT

28

The Transformative Power of Travel

One's destination is never a place, but a new way of seeing things.
—HENRY MILLER

The seeker of Mastery is a traveler. And travel, for our purposes, has a distinct connotation. It means observing and learning, being open to fresh new wonders that fire your imagination.

It means being an explorer.

What we commonly consider travel takes many forms— business excursions, tourism, cruises, group events, vacations—but you can shorten the list. Start by tossing "vacations" into the same trash bin where you dumped other flawed concepts like "retirement" and "elderly" and "act your age." Ditto for "tourism," which you can replace with "exploration." Instead of being a tourist, visitor, or sightseer at exotic locales, you can embark on missions of *discovery*.

The ultimate reward of such missions is the discovery of self.

> *We shall not cease from exploration, and the end of all our exploring will be to arrive where we started and know the place for the first time.*
> — T. S. ELIOT, *Four Quartets*

Travel has the power to transform you. Each time you depart the well worn path that you tread each day, you gain a fresh opportunity to learn and grow. Each new horizon you explore connects you to a wider range of experiences.

And yet, for multitudes of would-be travelers, the open road is intimidating. Why? For the answer, look around you. Observe your contemporaries, especially those your age. How many are active travelers? Who among them has maintained an ongoing curiosity about foreign lands? Which of them exhibits a passion for learning new customs, cultures, languages?

The number, you may notice, is dwindling. Something has happened as they age. Their spirit of adventure is shadowed by a gnawing insecurity. Inertia overtakes them. They become increasingly reluctant to leave familiar surroundings. The prospect of venturing into the unknown daunts them as it never did before. They worry about hypothetical calamities.

- *What if I get sick?*
- *What if something happens to my [fill in the blank] ... spouse, kids, house, business, pets, investments ... while I'm away?*
- *What if I miss my plane?*
- *What if my reservation gets lost?*
- *What if I get ... [fill in the blank] mugged, lost, stranded, bored, hassled, ignored, detained?*

The what-ifs pile up like unpaid bills. Here's another what-if. What if you stopped worrying about the what-ifs? What if you came up with a mini-plan for the realistic contingencies—the ones that concern health, family, and livelihood. Write the mini-plans down. Then place them in a file and press on.

Life is finite. The road beckons.

But wait, you say. What if something *else* happens? Something you missed on the list of contingencies. You know, something awful like ...

Stuff happens, good and bad, whether you travel or not. For the bad stuff you may consider purchasing a traveler's policy, obtainable from most travel agents. Depending on your age and any pre-existing conditions, you'll find this kind of temporary coverage to be surprisingly affordable. Most insurers cover not only medical expenses but the cost of emergency evacuation and compensate you for trip interruption. Check out companies like Travel Guard, Seven Corners, or HTH Worldwide who specialize in travel insurance packages tailored for U. S. citizens heading overseas.

All travel calamities are not equal. Most, like missed connections, dropped reservations, lost luggage turn out to be, in retrospect, less calamitous than they seemed. To worry about them in advance is to unnecessarily subtract from the quality of your experience. Travel is a metaphor for life. Not always predictable, sometimes messy, filled with surprises.

Is it worth the journey? Emphatically, yes.

But, you ask, what about the hassle? Can't international travel be an excruciating ordeal? You know all too well the godawfulness of airport security, the haughtiness of immigration officials, the zoned-out bone-weariness you felt after a trans-ocean flight. And you remember the stress you felt when your plans went off the rails and you didn't know what would happen next? Sure, you're intimidated by the unknown.

Some of these are valid concerns. Travel, like life, is seldom a smooth passage without turbulence. Flights *are* sometimes cancelled. Hotels *do* botch reservations. Tsunamis, earthquakes, floods, riots, even wars happen. And the fatigue of crossing oceans and time zones is real. It goes with the territory. Consider these aspects of travel as tiny speed bumps on the road to your destination.

The art of traveling well requires being flexible. It means adapting to the environment, learning to grab naps, knowing how to relax, to hoard creative energy, to slip through time zones with minimum grogginess.

If you're a senior adult, this could actually be the *best* time in life to hit the road. Hassles and delays and cancellations don't impact you like they used to. No kids to get back to school. No job demanding your presence on Monday morning. No PTA events, business appointments, sales meetings you can't miss.

You're free. Schedule upsets can flow past you like the natural current of a stream. Instead of being frustrated, you can regard a delay as an opportunity for new adventure. It's a chance to get acquainted with fellow travelers, jot impressions in your notebook, contemplate the reason for your journey.

Ah, yes, the *reason*. With the what-ifs addressed and stuffed in the bin where they belong, you can ask: *Why* travel? What reason do *you* have for breaking out of your comfort zone and journeying beyond your shores?

Several, actually. Here are a few:

— *Because you become a collector of rare moments.*

You are intrigued by new tastes, different ideas, unfamiliar cultures. Like a child seeing your first elephant, you gaze with jaw-dropping awe at each new wonderment. The need to travel comes as naturally as the desire to acquire new skills.

— *Because your viewpoint shifts.*

When you leave behind your familiar surroundings and immerse yourself in a foreign culture, something happens. Your brain goes into a receptive mode. You see your world—and yourself—in a different light. That wide-eyed, open-ended, wonderment-seeking journey of discovery has the power to alter your perceptions.

— *Because traveling means learning.*

And observing. It means venturing beyond the bus tours and cruise ship stopovers and guided walks. You, the Master traveler seek the alien, the bizarre, the unique. You *experience* with all your senses the sights and flavors and pulse of your destination. You are interested not just in the physical properties of what you have experienced, you seek its *meaning*. You record your impressions in your notebooks and journals and camera. And in so doing you make your own passage of discovery.

— *Because life is finite.*

You've heard this several times now. Keep remembering it. Make it a mantra. Stamp it on your subconscious. The time to travel to that destination you've been dreaming about is *now*.

The Solo Traveler

We travel because we need to, because distance and difference are the secret tonic of creativity. When we get home, home is still the same. But something in our mind has been changed, and that changes everything.
— JONAH LEHRER

Does the prospect of traveling alone seem unnatural? Intimidating? Dangerous? With no one to watch your back, who's going to deter predators? Help carry luggage? Share expenses? Translate menus? Make idle conversation at sidewalk cafes? Watch your bags while you go to the john? Keep you from being lonely?

Well, no one. No one but yourself. Embarking on a journey all by yourself may punch a large hole in the boundary of your comfort zone. But it may also open up a whole new vista of confidence. In the process of going it alone, you may discover a level of self-reliance you didn't know you possessed. You may find that *you* are your best traveling companion.

Why travel alone? For some it may be reasons of necessity—the loss of a loved one, or a need to exit a situation. But for the Master traveler, a solo expedition can be a journey of opportunity.

Here are reasons to consider traveling alone:
— *You make all the choices.*

> Groups, even couples, rarely agree on a trip agenda, but you, the solo traveler, are a free agent. No vote-taking about where to stay, when to leave, what to see. Democracy be damned. You linger as long as you wish in the Impressionist wing of the museum. You impulsively jump on that odd-numbered tram to the intriguing seaside village. You dart into that café with the intoxicating fragrance of dark java. You veer off the hiking trail to check out that little lodge. Your call. No questions asked.

— *You can reflect on what's most important to you.*

> This is not a cliché. Being alone in a foreign destination provides a unique viewpoint for solving problems. Sitting in an oriental park, perched at a Parisian sidewalk café, encamped on the shore of an alpine lake—all are suitable venues for writing in your notebook, meditating, reading that book you'd never take the time for if you weren't alone.

— *You meet new people.*

> Which may seem obvious, but it's not. Traveling with multiple companions makes it harder to interact with both locals and other travelers. A shell goes up around groups that tends to buffer them from other people. The solo traveler is much more free to mingle with locals, strike up conversations, experience the locale in a way that isn't likely when traveling with a group.

— *You experience more.*

By not being focused on companions, not engaged in ongoing conversation and the sharing of perceptions, you are more open to the sights and sounds and flavors of your destination. You are free to be a gatherer of impressions. You learn more.

— *You can enjoy your own company.*

Unless loneliness is an unbearable burden for you, luxuriate in listening to your own thoughts. Be selfish. As writer Andrew O'Hagan put it, "The first rule of travel is that you should always go with someone you love, which is why I travel alone."

— *You gain new confidence.*

Something happens when the realization strikes you: *I did this on my own.* You will take a secret pleasure in navigating through the labyrinth of a new city. You may have taken a wrong metro, misread a map, overpaid for a taxi, but you rose to the occasion. You acquired a new sense of self-reliance. It's a sweet feeling. The feeling of Mastery.

Travel is more than the seeing of sights; it is a change that goes on, deep and permanent, in the ideas of living.
—MIRIAM BEARD

For sure, solo travel isn't for everyone. Those with physical impairments may not be up to arduous trips with multiple check in-check outs and airport drills. Very senior travelers may require the assistance of a companion. For them a better plan is to establish a suitable base station—hotel, vessel, B&B—from which they can make forays into the foreign landscape.

But the number one reason given for *not* traveling solo is almost always the same: safety. Being safe means being smart. The adventure of traveling on your own doesn't have to be dangerous or difficult. Do your homework, be informed about your destination, know where it is safe to go and where the limits are. Some destinations are more suitable than others for the lone traveler.

Traveling alone doesn't have to mean *being* alone. Consider signing up for guided walking tours or cooking classes or snorkeling trips. You're sure to meet other travelers, and most love talking about where they're from, what they've seen, where they've been.

And engage the locals. Ask questions. Even if you're an introvert back home, interacting with local people is the best and most rewarding way to learn the *real* culture of your destination.

Again, travel is a metaphor for life. Trust your intuition. When a person or place or situation doesn't feel right, extricate yourself. When moving about in public in a foreign city, present an assertive posture. Stay alert, confident, and be rude if necessary. So as not to tempt thieves, leave flashy jewelry, expensive accouterments and fashion statements at home. Avoid discussing details about yourself with strangers—where you're staying, whom you're with, where you're going. Know your route and stay in open, public spaces. Try not to arrive in a new location after dark. Order taxis from a hotel concierge instead of on the street.

The solo traveler should maintain a situational awareness. The Canadian writer Janice Waugh is a widow, empty-nester, and traveler who writes the *Solo Traveler* blog. "Stay in public," is her first rule of solo travel safety. "Be informed about your destination. Study maps before you arrive so that you know where it is safe to go and where the limits of safety lie." And, Waugh counsels both men and women, "Keep perspective on what's important: your person, your documents, your money, and your stuff—in that order."

The U. S. State Department offers a free program called STEP (Smart Traveler Enrollment Program). They issue timely, country-specific alerts and warnings and allow you to designate an emergency contact person. STEP will help you out of a jam in case of a natural disaster, war crisis, or a personal calamity like lost passport, and will facilitate contacting family members back home.

Another good way to cover your backside is to email copies of all important travel documents to yourself. Try to travel with more than one credit card in case one doesn't work for any reason. Alert your credit card issuers that you will be out of the country so they won't cancel your card when the multiple foreign transactions start showing up. Carry with you the emergency contacts for all your credit card issuers in case you need a quick replacement.

Slow Down

> I don't want to hurry it. That itself is a poisonous twentieth-century attitude. When you want to hurry something, that means you no longer care about it and want to get on to other things.
> —ROBERT M. PIRSIG, *Zen and the Art of Motorcycle Maintenance*

If there's anything that squeezes the joy from the journey, it's pressure—usually self-inflicted—to cram as much into the experience as you can. It's a natural impulse. You're on a time-constrained trip and you feel compelled to see it all—the museums, shows, ruins, markets, natural wonders. And it rushes past in a blur. At the end of each day you have difficulty distinguishing one brief exposure from another. Instead of making the most of your time, you've spent your precious hours in a torrent of mini-experiences.

To rush through a travel experience, pressuring yourself to *do* as many sights and cities and countries as time allows is to stay bound to a schedule. You're constantly aware of the upcoming end of your journey. You're missing out on the prime reward of leaving home—the transformative power of travel.

Here's a better way: shorten your agenda. Try to live in the moment with your attention focused on what you're seeing, doing, feeling *now*. Don't rush it. Stop, get off the bus, sit on a bench, take a walk, watch and listen, stand for as long as you like gazing in awe at an object of wonder. Let yourself be entertained by simple novelties and oddments. Let your inner child's curiosity take over.

Which happens to be a good reason for traveling on your own, making your own schedule, rather than joining a packaged tour or cruise ship stopover. Being swept along in a gaggle of tourists behind a guide may rob you of the chance to take your time and connect with your locale.

Slow down. Smell the tulips. Haggle in the market. Stroll through the ancient ruins. Admire the sunset. Savor your freedom. In so doing, you'll be more relaxed, more receptive to learning, more attuned to the pulse and rhythm of your surrounding.

The Journey: What Did It Mean?

By keeping a record you deepen the travel, you become more aware of what's happening as you record it in the evening or the next morning, whatever it happens to be.
— WILLIAM LEAST HEAT-MOON

Each day take the time to reflect on your journey. Find a quiet place and a still moment. Have a conversation with yourself. Review in your mind your recent experience.

What did you find most agreeable? Most disagreeable?

How have your perceptions of this place and culture altered?

What surprised you?

How have the day's happenings affected you?

What did it mean?

And then write it down. Make writing in your journal as much a part of your traveling life as snapping photographs and reading guidebooks. Capture your impressions. Let them become a part of you. In this way you grow. You take another step on the route to Mastery.

ROBERT GANDT AND GARY A. SCOTT

29

Missions Great and Small

So you're ready to assign yourself a mission. You've decided you want to insert *purpose* into your daily existence. You want your life to be *about* something.

Where to start?

Missions come in all dimensions and degrees of difficulty. You could begin with something short and accomplishable. You could train for a ten-kilometer race. Learn to make world-class Gazpacho. Lose twenty pounds. Build a Zen garden. These are missions of modest scope.

Or you may consider a megamission, which is an undertaking of Homeric proportions. Think of Jeff Bezos's mission to revolutionize the way books are marketed and read. Think of Jonas Salk's mission to develop a polio vaccine. Think of Jacque Cousteau's mission to save the endangered oceans.

Here are examples of megamissions:

— Deliver clean water to a third world country
— Start a foundation to prevent teenage pregnancy
— Provide mentoring to inner city children
— Stop illegal killing of elephants
— Save sharks from annihilation
— Preserve a rain forest

Megamissions are undertaken by strivers possessed with an all-consuming passion. Their personal lives are subordinated to the pursuit of their mission. Most of the great achievers—inventors, industry magnates, explorers, reformers—were pursuers of mega missions. It should be noted that the crash and burn rate for megamissions is perilously high.

Not ready for a megamission? That's okay. Few of us are. But missions, mega or otherwise, are scalable, which is to say you can apply your own parameters. Don't want to climb Mt. Everest? Consider training for a trek up a promontory in your state. Don't feel like going into combat against ivory poachers in Africa? Start a foundation to help save an endangered species.

Here are examples of grand missions that can be scaled to more accomplishable alternatives.

Mission . . . .   **Alternative Mission**

Write a best-selling book . . . .   Publish a magazine article

Become a performing musician . . . .   Learn to play a musical instrument

Sail a boat across an ocean. . . . .   Learn to sail a boat

Fly an airplane across the U. S. . . . .   Earn a pilot's license

Hike the entire Appalachian Trail . . . . .   Make a week long trek

Compete in an Ironman competition . . .Train for a sprint triathlon

Race in a marathon . . . .   Run a 10 kilometer race

Speak a foreign language fluently . . . . .   Learn basic Spanish or French or Italian.

Ride a bicycle across America . . . .   Train for a hundred mile
bike event

Discover an ancient shipwreck . . . .   Learn to scuba dive

The list is endless. Notice how many of the alternative examples begin with "Learn." That's because learning is the essence of Mastery. Learning is growing. Only by continuing to learn will you continue to advance as a human being.

Regardless of the mission you choose, it won't have substance until you give it the structure of a mission plan.

In case you've forgotten, here again are the elements of a typical mission plan:

— *An objective (What)*

— *A strategy (How)*

— *Interim goals (Waypoints toward the objective)*

— *A time frame (When)*

Given a well defined plan, you may now evaluate whether the mission is right for you. Is it worth the cost in time? Energy? Money? Does it claim your passion? Does it stir an old yearning inside you?

If the answer is yes, then there's only one step left. You know what it is. Give it your full commitment.

Ready for lift off? Congratulations. You're about to commence your journey to Mastery. We wish you huge success.

About the Authors

credit: Anne Busse-Gandt

ROBERT GANDT is a former naval officer, international airline captain, and an award-winning military and aviation writer. He is the author of more than a dozen books, including the novels *The Killing Sky*, *The President's Pilot,* and the definitive work on modern naval aviation, *Bogeys and Bandits.* His screen credits include the television series *Pensacola: Wings of Gold.* His acclaimed account of the Battle for Okinawa, *The Twilight Warriors* (Broadway Books, 2010) was the winner of the Samuel Eliot Morison Award for Naval Literature. He and his wife, Anne, live in the Spruce Creek Fly-In, an aviation community in Daytona Beach, Florida. For reviews and excerpts from all his books, visit the author's website at www.gandt.com.

credit: Merri Scott

Gary A. Scott's book, *Passport to International Profit*, was one of America's first publications to suggest global investing in the 1970s. Gary has written a newsletter about gaining health and wealth globally since. He has appeared on numerous TV and radio shows and was heard weekly on the syndicated radio program, Market Rap, broadcast by WEVD in New York City. His monthly column "The Global Guru" appeared for years in *On Wall Street*, one of the largest circulation magazines for US stock brokers. He and his wife, Merri, live in Florida and the Blue Ridge Mountains and publish daily notes about investing in value at http://www.garyscott.com.

Made in the USA
Charleston, SC
24 October 2015